# George Washington *and* ALEXANDRIA

# George Washington *and* ALEXANDRIA

## *A Founding Friendship*

TIM ROSE

Published by The History Press
An imprint of Arcadia Publishing
Charleston, SC
www.historypress.com



First published 2026

Manufactured in the United States

ISBN 9781467170642

Library of Congress Control Number applied for.

# CONTENTS

# PREFACE

It was a somber day in 1785 when George Washington walked next to the casket of his friend William Ramsay. In one of his few public acts as a Freemason, Washington marched in a funeral procession, performing "Masonic rites." Washington was a member of the local Freemason Lodge formed in Alexandria that is today known as the Alexandria-Washington Lodge No. 22. On the day that Washington joined in the funeral procession, he gathered with many Alexandrians to mourn the loss of one of their most prominent citizens and former mayor, William Ramsay.

George Washington's friendship with Ramsay extended back to his late teenage years. Ramsay, along with a handful of other Scottish merchants, helped create the town of Alexandria. Ramsay was an early trustee, which referred to the system of government that was essentially an oligarchy of town landowners. Ramsay bought two half-acre lots in Alexandria on the waterfront when Alexandria was founded on July 13, 1749.

Ramsay's former residence has been rebuilt in the heart of Alexandria's Old and Historic District and currently houses the Alexandria Visitor Center. Popular legend claims that the house is the oldest in Alexandria, having been built around 1724. The story of how the house was built twenty-five years before Ramsay owned the property speaks to the fact that the house was originally in Dumfries, Virginia, which is about thirty miles south of Alexandria. The house was disassembled in Dumfries, barged in pieces up the Potomac River, and reassembled in Alexandria.

The William Ramsay House, originally owned by Alexandria founder, William Ramsay, and later reconstructed after a 1940s fire, now serves as the city's visitor center. *Photo by the author.*

Ramsay and his family developed a strong bond with George Washington that is emblematic of Washington's relationship with his friends and neighbors in Alexandria. During the French and Indian War, Ramsay relied on Washington's support financially. After the war, Washington leaned on Ramsay for financial assistance. Both men obliged the other without hesitation. This generosity culminated in George Washington agreeing to pay for Ramsay's son to pursue an education at the College of New Jersey, now Princeton University, at an annual tuition cost of twenty-five pounds. In a letter to Ramsay dated January 29, 1769, Washington wrote that he did not wish for anything in return. He said, "No other return is expected or wished for." Washington further hoped that Ramsay would "accept [the offer] with the same freedom & good will with which it is made."[1] Washington biographer Douglas Southall Freeman describes the passage as "the most generous sentence that had ever come from [George Washington's] pen."[2]

In 1785, the affection was solidified by Washington's honoring of Ramsay at his funeral. It was the same year that Washington collaborated with other leading citizens of Alexandria to start the Alexandria Academy. In doing so, Washington continued to play the part of benefactor to children of Alexandria seeking an education just as he had done with William Ramsay's son in 1769.

As a result, when another one of William Ramsay's sons, Dennis Ramsay, was mayor of Alexandria in 1789, he offered a moving tribute to George Washington that praised Washington as a benefactor and supporter of education in Alexandria. However, what is noteworthy about Dennis Ramsay's praise was that it occurred on April 16, 1789. On this day, Dennis Ramsay toasted George Washington at a tavern in Alexandria run by John Wise. It was Washington's first public appearance after receiving news of his election as president of the United States on April 14. Two weeks later, Washington was inaugurated in New York City on April 30. However, Mayor Dennis Ramsay was the first public official to honor the newly elected President Washington in a public gathering. Thus, the city of Alexandria was the first city to celebrate Washington's election with him and send him off to serve his country as America's first president.

# Introduction

## A FOUNDING FRIENDSHIP

No city can claim a closer connection to George Washington than the city of Alexandria.* It is not surprising, considering the proximity of Alexandria to Mount Vernon. While Mount Vernon was Washington's home, Alexandria was his hometown. Washington may not have used these words explicitly. However, George Washington would not have achieved his success without Alexandria and the people who helped create and build the city.

The city of Alexandria was formally established in 1749 when George Washington was seventeen years old. Both Alexandria's founding and George Washington's coming of age happened simultaneously. While Alexandria grew, Washington grew with it. Their fortunes were intimately tied to each other and forged through the hardship of war and the challenges of peace. As a result, Washington's connections to Alexandria provide an exceptional perspective on his life, leadership, and legacy.

In exploring Washington's connections to Alexandria, it is important to understand that many Alexandrians were born before the city was founded in 1749. Many Alexandrians were first-generation Americans. To say that Alexandria supported George Washington means the people who claimed it as home whether they were founders like William Ramsay or later residents

---

* Alexandria was first established as a town in 1749 but officially became a city in 1779. Throughout the book, specific references prior to 1779 will describe Alexandria as a town. References to Alexandria after 1779 will describe it as a city. In discussing Alexandria generally, it will be described as a city.

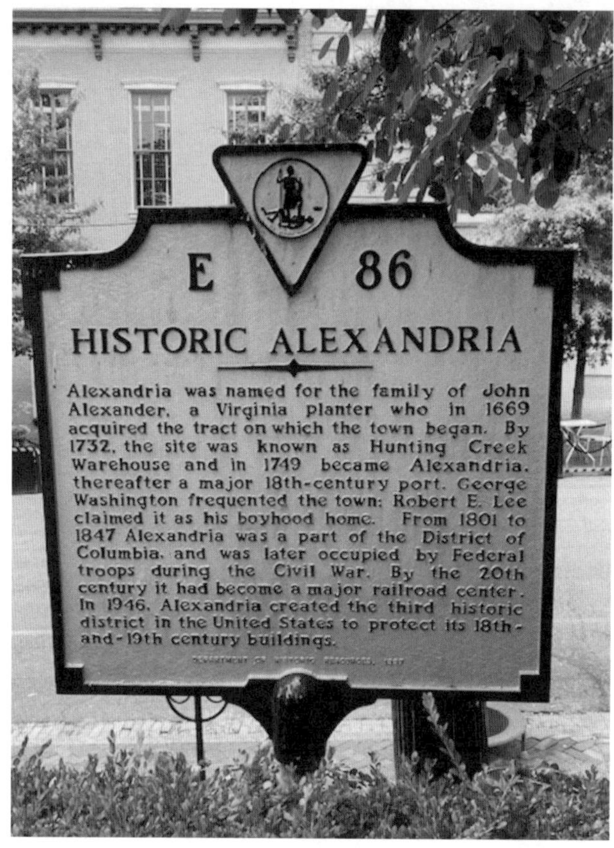


This historic marker outside the Alexandria Visitor Center provides an overview of the city's past for visitors to Old Town. *Photo by the author.*

like Dr. James Craik. As a result, the number of Alexandrians who supported Washington throughout his life is a lengthy list of people that provided the backbone of an extensive network.

Washington is a great man of history, whose incredible leadership traits and abilities can be explored through his military service, business acumen, and political influence, as well as his personal relationships. Like all good leaders, Washington did not command the stage alone. Washington would not have been "His Excellency General George Washington" without the support of his friends and family. While his network was not exclusive to Alexandria, Washington's Alexandria family and friends were the most influential of any other network in Washington's life. It is that friendship with a city and its people that enabled his success from the moment he left home to pursue his own personal and professional ambitions in 1748 until the day he died in December 1799.

# Chapter 1

# AN AUSPICIOUS BEGINNING

George Washington was born on February 11, 1731, based on the Julian or Old-Style calendar. When he was twenty, the British adopted the Gregorian-style calendar, which shifted the date to February 22, 1732. Washington was born in Westmoreland County, Virginia, in a simple frame house adjacent to Popes Creek, which connected to the Potomac River. Washington's birth year coincided with the first major piece of commercial infrastructure that would birth the city of Alexandria. After the passage of the Tobacco Inspection Act in 1730, a tobacco inspection warehouse was built along Alexandria's waterfront by 1732. The warehouse was constructed on a piece of shoreline that stretched into the deep-water portion of the Potomac River and became known as West's Point. Hugh West owned the land, ran the warehouse, and established a tavern at that location.

Over the next sixteen years, George Washington lived in several places. When Washington was three years old, the family moved to Little Hunting Creek onto a property that would eventually be called Mount Vernon. In 1738, Washington's family moved to Ferry Farm across the Rappahannock River from the town of Fredericksburg.

George Washington spent much of his youth at Ferry Farm. He received a basic education, but not the formal schooling that was afforded to his older half brothers Lawrence and Augustine Jr. Both brothers were related through his father, Augustine Washington, whose first marriage was to Jane Butler. After Butler's death in 1729, Augustine married Mary Ball. Their first child was George. They would have five other children. George outlived them all.

Pope's Creek in Westmoreland County, Virginia, the birthplace of George Washington in 1732. *Photo by the author.*

Washington's father, Augustine Washington, died in 1743, when George was eleven. In the absence of a father figure, Washington's older half brothers became mentors and role models to young George. Washington biographer Douglas Freeman described Lawrence as George's "best friend."[3] Lawrence was also a veteran of Britain's war against Spain called the War of Jenkins' Ear (1739–48). On June 9, 1740, Lawrence received a commission from King George II and was a captain in one of four companies formed under the Virginia Foot Regiments.[4] As a boy, George adored his half brother Captain Lawrence Washington.

Lawrence served in a naval flotilla during the Cartagena Campaign. Captain Lawrence Washington experienced grueling service with little action. However, he was impressed by the leadership of his commanding officer, Admiral Edward Vernon. Lawrence's service ended in 1742. In the following year, 1743, Augustine Washington died. As a result, Lawrence inherited the property his father had purchased along with the four-room house built on Little Hunting Creek. After the ownership was transferred to Lawrence, he renamed the Little Hunting Creek property after his commanding officer, Admiral Vernon. Thus, the property was christened "Mount Vernon." George, who was then eleven years old, would keep the name when the property was officially transferred to him in 1761.

While Lawrence's military service was laudatory, George may have been more impressed by his personal success, specifically his marriage to Anne Fairfax. The Fairfax family of Belvoir Plantation was one of the wealthiest and most prestigious in Virginia. Lord Thomas Fairfax, Sixth Baron of Cameron, had obtained a series of land titles that gave him possession of 5,282,000 acres in Virginia. Lord Fairfax's cousin, Colonel William Fairfax, was the land agent who helped manage and monetize the vast landholdings.

William Fairfax was born in Yorkshire, England, in 1691. He was a former Royal Navy officer who lived for several years in Massachusetts until he was hired by his cousin Lord Thomas Fairfax in 1734. William Fairfax then moved south to Westmoreland County, Virginia, before relocating his family to a new site along the Potomac River in 1738. In 1741, he built Belvoir Manor on the Potomac River property, which neighbored the property that was soon to be called Mount Vernon. Thus, upon his return to Virginia from the Cartagena Campaign and his inheritance of Mount Vernon in 1743, Lawrence Washington got to know his new neighbors, the Fairfax family of Belvoir. As an eligible bachelor, Lawrence sought and received Anne Fairfax's hand in marriage.

For George Washington, his brother's marriage to Anne changed the course of his life. George was now a "welcome visitor at Belvoir."[5] He was in the orbit of the most powerful people in Virginia. In fact, the union of the Washington and Fairfax family formed a political juggernaut in Virginia. Lawrence and his father-in-law, Colonel William Fairfax, served in the House of Burgesses representing Fairfax County. Lawrence became adjutant general for the Northern Virginia military district. In 1748, Colonel William Fairfax became head of the King's Council, which made him de facto lieutenant governor with one of the most influential political roles in Virginia.

Washington biographer Ron Chernow describes Colonel Fairfax as Washington's "stalwart patron" and claims that George was "tutored by Lawrence and the Fairfax family."[6] At the same time, the strong partnership of son-in-law and father-in-law was equally critical for the fortunes of a town soon to be created with the name of Alexandria. Mount Vernon was adjacent to where Little Hunting Creek fed into the Potomac River. Several miles north, another body of water called Great Hunting Creek also flowed into the Potomac River. Lawrence's attention was drawn to this upstart area where commercial activity was tied to Virginia's thriving tobacco economy.

By the early 1740s, the tobacco inspection warehouses in Alexandria had attracted additional settlement and economic development around what was known as the Hunting Creek Warehouse. The location of the warehouses was promising along a wide and deep-water portion of the Potomac River. Alexandria's geographic location was also important below the Great Falls or Potomac River fall line. The Great Falls were impassable for large ships, and Alexandria became a strategic location upriver where a deep-water port could be established.

Lawrence had a vision in 1748 that a town was needed north of his Mount Vernon property. However, the year 1748 was no accident, since it followed the organization of the Ohio Company in which Lawrence and Colonel Fairfax were directors and investors.[7] The company claimed 500,000 acres in the Ohio River Valley, which was then part of the vast wilderness of the

American western frontier. Alexandria was conceived as a port town where crops from the western frontier could be exported while goods from abroad could be imported. Alexandria was destined to be a critical hub in a network of global trade. With its tobacco warehouses and growing merchant class, Lawrence saw potential in the area that locals were already referring to as Belhaven, which honored the Scottish Earl of Belhaven.

In 1748, Lawrence petitioned the Virginia general assembly to authorize the creation of a town north of Great Hunting Creek along the Potomac River. Colonel Fairfax also supported the effort, bringing the Fairfax influence into the petition. Lawrence and Colonel Fairfax were successful. On May 2, 1749, the Virginia House of Burgesses approved the creation of Alexandria. The town was carved from sixty acres owned by the descendants of John Alexander from a land patent that dated back to 1669. Two months later, the town of Alexandria was formally established when the first of eighty-four half-acre lots were sold at an auction that began on July 13, 1749. The land was sold for Spanish pistoles, and the money went to John Alexander's descendants. Thus, the name changed from Belhaven to Alexandria in honor of the Alexanders.

Lawrence and Colonel Fairfax's work in the formation of Alexandria occurred simultaneously with their influence over George Washington's career. Originally, they made plans to send George into the navy as a midshipman. However, those plans were foiled by Washington's mother, Mary Ball, who ended the idea as soon as she caught discussion of it. However, there was an alternative to a career at sea. There were lucrative prospects on the land, specifically in the profession of surveyor. Surveying was ideal work for an athletic, active, and enterprising young man. Colonel William Fairfax employed surveyors to transform his cousin's 5.2 million acres into a profitable, cash flow–producing asset. Although he did not attend college, young George was strong in mathematics and was already learning the trade of surveying with equipment left by his late father. His curiosity, hard work ethic, and physical abilities made him a natural fit for work as a surveyor.

In March 1748, George was sixteen years old when he embarked on his first survey for the Fairfax family. He joined Colonel Fairfax's son, George William Fairfax, who became one of Washington's best friends. Washington's 1748 survey was a crash course in the profession and one that he documented in "A Journal of My Journey Over the Mountains." His first survey expedition concluded around the time Lawrence brought his idea to the Virginia House of Burgesses for the town of Alexandria. As a result,

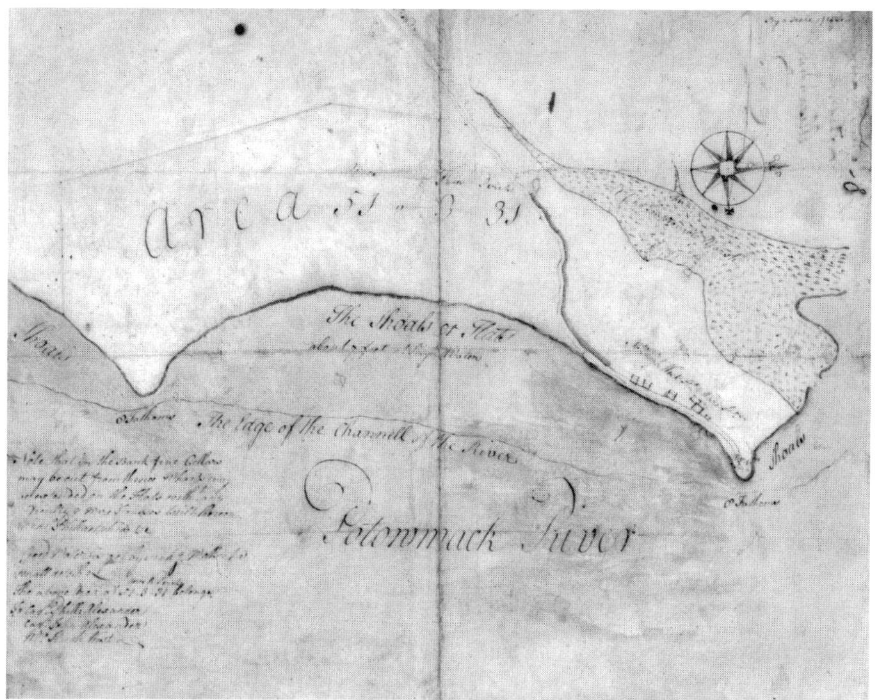


George Washington's 1748 survey map of Alexandria, completed when he was just sixteen years old. *Library of Congress.*

George drew one of the first surveys for the town as early as 1748. By 1749, George Washington was still learning the trade of surveying and drew yet another survey map of Alexandria. Both survey maps Washington copied from the town's lead surveyor, John West Jr. Both maps are still available at the Library of Congress.

Many people have tried to credit Washington as the surveyor of Alexandria. In doing so, they have overemphasized Washington's role in the creation of Alexandria and underemphasized the impact that Alexandria had on young George Washington. We can conclude that Washington had a role in surveying Alexandria and even suggest that it was not insignificant. However, what is more important is how Washington's survey of Alexandria effectively launched his surveyor career and led to a meteoric rise for a young man in his late teens. Due to his Fairfax connections and work with the Alexandria survey, Washington was selected as surveyor for Culpeper County on July 20, 1749.[8] In the book *Washington Entrepreneur*, author John Berlau writes that Washington conducted two hundred surveys over three years for private clients and made an estimated £400, which was nearly four

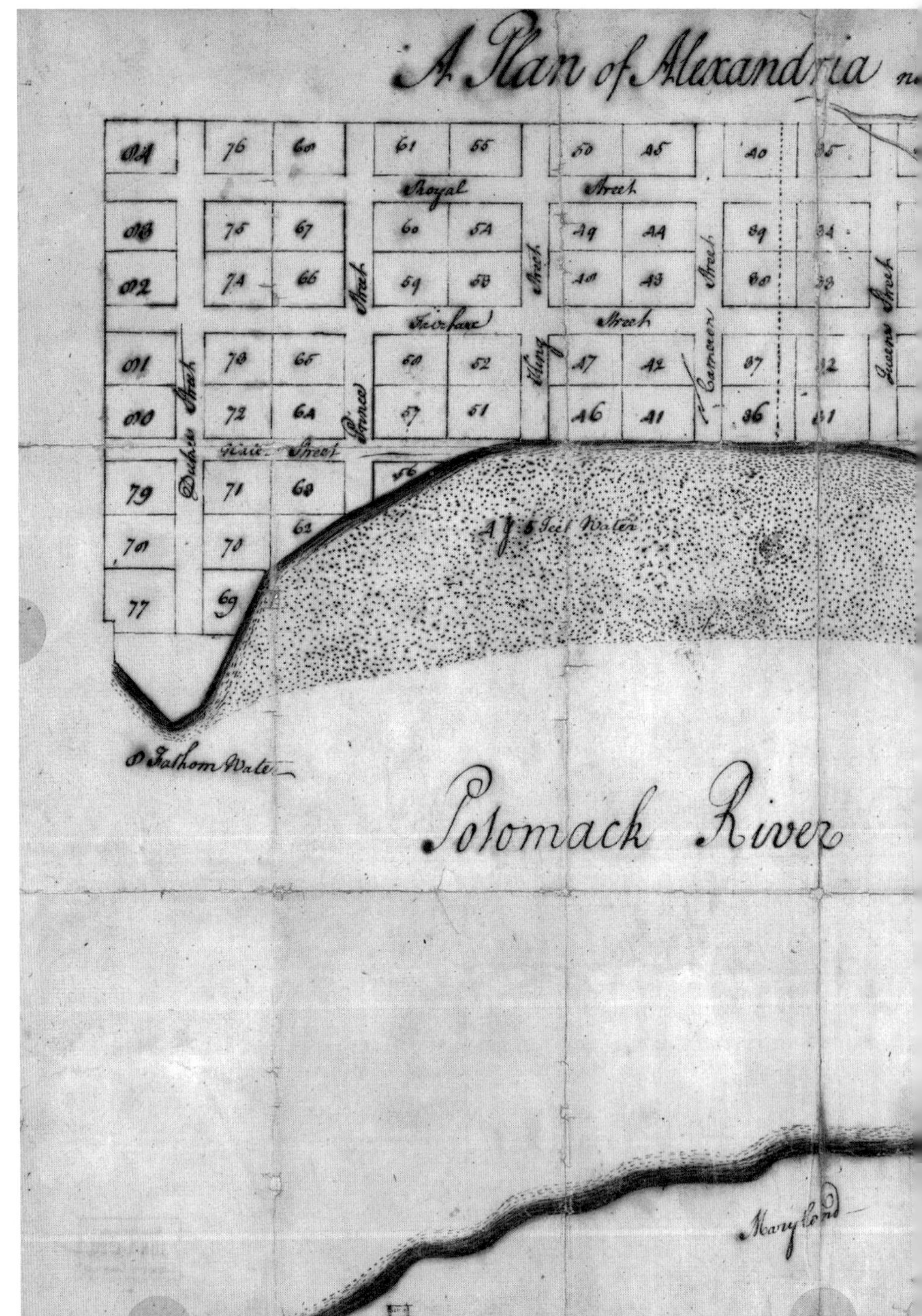

A Plan of Alexandria
Royal Street
Fairfax Street
Duke Street
Prince Street
King Street
Cameron Street
Queen Street
Water Street
8 Fathom Water
Potomack River
Maryland

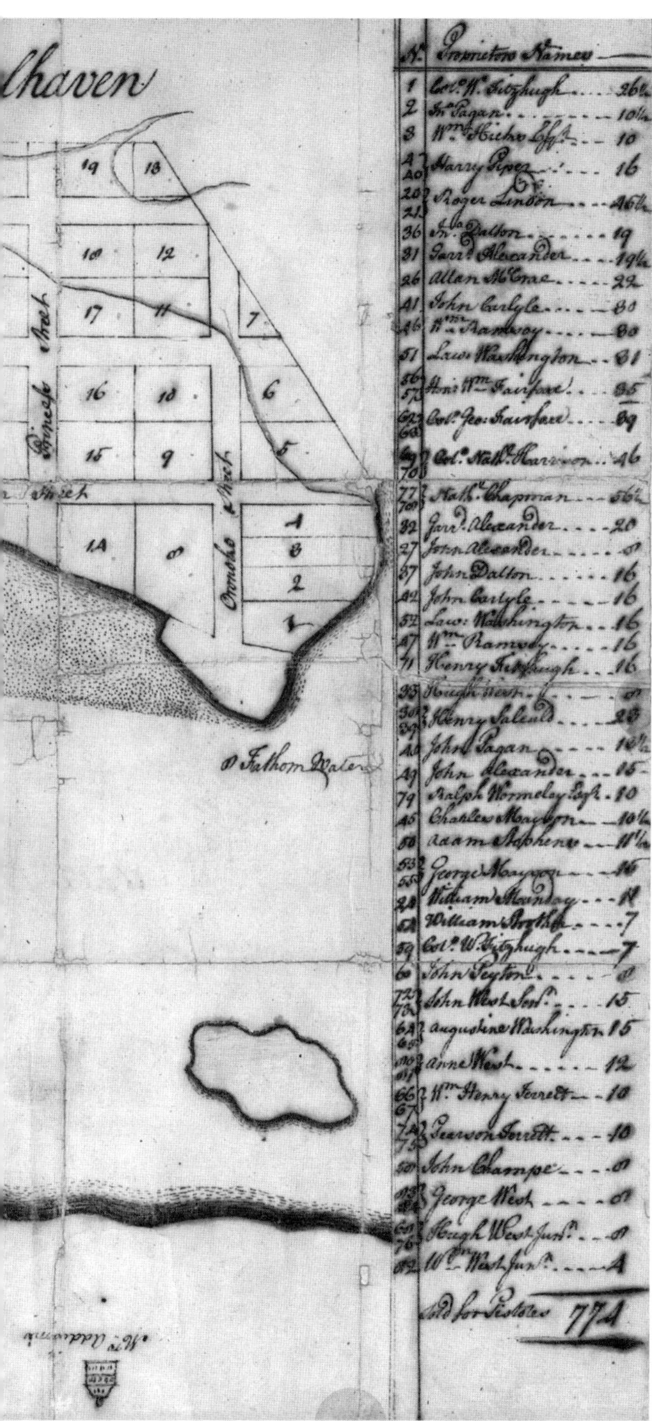


George Washington's 1749 survey map of Alexandria, created the year the town was founded. *Library of Congress.*

times the annual earnings of a skilled craftsman.[9] Berlau continues, "Still in his late teens, Washington was suddenly earning more from surveying in a few months than many Virginia farmers and merchants made in a year."[10]

Washington's 1749 Alexandria survey map is very detailed. It shows the exact plats of eighty-four half-acre lots with seven streets running east–west and three running north–south. The street layouts today remain consistent with Washington's early survey map. The map also includes a list of the buyers and how much they paid in Spanish pistoles. Both of Washington's older half brothers, Lawrence and Augustine Jr., are included on the list. Colonel Fairfax is also on the list, along with notable merchants such as John Carlyle, William Ramsay, and John Dalton. George Mason of Gunston Hall was also one of the first property owners in Alexandria. Mason had joined with Lawrence and Colonel Fairfax in the Ohio Company. He became a trustee of Alexandria as well.

Finally, it has also been asserted that Washington's copy of the Alexandria survey map was drawn specifically for his brother Lawrence. Lawrence bought lots 51 and 52. Lot 51 was specifically on the shoreline along what used to be known as Water Street (now Lee Street). Colonel Fairfax bough lot 57, which was on the same block as Lawrence's lots, and he also bought lot 56. Augustine Washington Jr. bought lots 64 and 65 on Prince Street. Finally, William Ramsay bought lots 46 and 47. Next to Ramsay, John Carlyle acquired lots 41 and 42. Finally, George Mason bought lots 53 and 55, which were on King Street.

Alexandria and its founding fathers had an outsized impact on young George Washington. The start of George Washington's professional career and Alexandria's creation went hand in hand. Both the young surveyor and young town could trace their origins to Lawrence Washington, whom George considered his "best friend." Furthermore, while he was a founder of Alexandria, Colonel Fairfax also became like a father figure to George Washington as well as his mentor and patron. Finally, it should be noted that George Washington looked up to and revered Lord Fairfax as well. George would maintain a proper reverence and respect for Lord Fairfax up until Fairfax's death in 1781. Nevertheless, by 1750, both the new town of Alexandria and young Washington had big aspirations. They would soon be at the center of momentous events in world history.

# Chapter 2

# THE DRUMS OF WAR

As Alexandria grew in the early 1750s, George Washington was also coming of age from a teenage boy into a broad-shoulder and physically imposing man. As a surveyor, Washington became adept at studying terrain and drawing maps. He endured hardships on the western frontier like sleeping in sheets ridden with lice and vermin. He interacted with Indian tribes and frontier settlers, gaining skills in diplomacy. Thus, Washington's surveying years were formative for him as a military officer. All of this would prove important as hostilities emerged between Britain and France over the Ohio River Valley.

Before Washington was called to military service, he suffered enormous personal tragedy when his half brother Lawrence died in 1752. Lawrence had struggled with tuberculosis since his service in the Cartagena Campaign. The illness was severe to the point that he left Virginia for the warmer climate of Barbados in 1751. On this trip, George accompanied him. It was the only time in George's life that he left America. It also proved to be a critical trip for George's own health. He contracted smallpox while in Barbados. Fortunately, his case of smallpox was not fatal. As inconvenient as it was in 1751, it was beneficial because Washington was now immunized against the virus. This was important especially during the Revolutionary War, when smallpox wreaked havoc on the American army.

Lawrence's death on July 26, 1752, was a tough loss for George. When Lawrence died, he was adjutant general in the northern neck district, one of four military districts in Virginia. Washington sought to replace his brother

Portrait of Lawrence Washington, George Washington's older half brother, who inherited Mount Vernon and helped shape George's early life. *Courtesy of Mount Vernon.*

as adjutant general. Lieutenant Governor Robert Dinwiddie commissioned Washington as adjutant general. However, he was appointed adjutant of the southern district rather than the northern neck district that he sought. Colonel Fairfax helped Washington secure the post in 1752. Colonel Fairfax was then head of the King's Council, which made him a critical advisor to Dinwiddie.

It is equally important to understand that Dinwiddie, like Lawrence and the Fairfaxes, was also an investor and actively involved in the Ohio Company. The mission of the Ohio Company was to develop land in the western territory of America in the Ohio River Valley, or Ohio Country as it was commonly named. The abundance of fertile land strategically placed along major waterways like the Ohio River and its tributaries held the promise of financial success for the Ohio Company and its principals.

But the Ohio Country attracted interest from other great powers that recognized its strategic importance and potential riches. Shortly after Lawrence died in 1752, the French made the first move to seize control of the Ohio Country. By 1753, they had mobilized military forces from Canada into the region of western Pennsylvania that would become the flashpoint of an international conflict.

As a result, the directors of the Ohio Company, including Governor Dinwiddie, sought to confront the French incursions while gaining a full picture of what the French were doing. Dinwiddie and Fairfax needed someone with physical stamina and courage to lead a mission that would be equal parts diplomatic and intelligence gathering. As a former surveyor of four years and a recently appointed adjutant general, George Washington was an ideal fit for the mission. Thus, on October 30, 1753, Dinwiddie "dispatched" Washington to "deliver my Letter [and] Message" to "the Commandant of the French Forces."[11] The contents of the sealed letter explained that the Ohio Country was claimed by the British and the French needed to vacate immediately. Furthermore, Dinwiddie wanted Washington to report back the strength of French forces in the Ohio Country. Washington accepted the mission, which would be his first official duties as a military officer at age twenty-one.

After receiving his commission as a major, Washington began his expedition. He kept a detailed journal of his travels to "visit & deliver a Letter to the Commandant of the French Forces on the Ohio."[12] On the first part of his journey, he met Jacob Van Braam, his interpreter, and "proceeded with him to Alexandria where we [were] provided Necessaries."[13] Alexandria and its merchant class quickly assumed a role of providing "necessaries"—the supplies and equipment that Washington would need to accomplish his mission. As George Washington arrived in Alexandria to begin his military career in 1753, both Washington and Alexandria joined together in a critical partnership that endured throughout the French and Indian War.

George Washington knew that the situation was dire. His mission across the Alleghany Mountains in 1753 gave him a firsthand look at French forces encroaching into the Ohio Country. Furthermore, Washington observed their plans being carried out to occupy the forks of the Ohio River. They were also making overtures to Indian tribes to secure critical alliances on the western frontier of North America.

Upon his return to Virginia, George Washington completed the journal about his experiences and presented it to Governor Dinwiddie. The journal of Major George Washington became a decisive account that proved the French were mobilizing to seize territory claimed by the British. It also showed Washington's attention to detail and was the equivalent of a military intelligence report. As a result, Governor Dinwiddie had Washington's journal published and distributed widely both in the colonies and in England. In the digital age, we might describe Washington's journal as "going viral." The analogy is appropriate because Washington's writings reached a massive audience and had major political and military implications. It also made George something of a celebrity by the time he was only twenty-two in 1754.

Word of what the French were doing in the Ohio River Valley circulated around Alexandria. In early 1754, the town was not yet five years old. However, like George Washington, the town was about to take center stage in a battle between global empires. For almost a decade (1753–63), the experience of a world war fundamentally transformed the destiny of George Washington, Alexandria, and America.

# Chapter 3

# A WORLD WAR BEGINS

John Carlyle came to Virginia with big ambitions. He was born in England in 1720 but had family ties to Scotland. Carlyle had an elder brother, George, who inherited much of the family fortune from their father, William Carlyle.[14] George also had an advantage over John in that he was educated at a prestigious university in Holland.[15] Thus, when John Carlyle moved to Virginia in 1741, he was determined to prove that the younger brother in the family could amount to something great. When he arrived in Virginia, Carlyle worked as a "factor" for a tobacco firm based in Whitehaven, England, and a boss named William Hicks. A factor was the equivalent of a sales agent. Carlyle's job was to build relationships with tobacco planters in Virginia, purchase tobacco, and have it shipped back to William Hicks in Whitehaven. By the time Alexandria was founded in 1749, Carlyle was doing well and had ambitions to become an independent merchant with his own firm and not a factor under a large European firm.

While Carlyle was hardworking and industrious, he did something that many young men in his position did when they wanted to accelerate their careers and fortunes: he married up! In fact, like Lawrence Washington, Carlyle married into the Fairfax family. Lawrence's wife, Anne Fairfax, had a sister, Sarah Fairfax. On December 31, 1747, Carlyle and Sarah Fairfax married. As Carlyle prepared for his marriage, he wrote a letter to his brother George, who was living in England. In the letter, John Carlyle explained how beneficial his marriage would be to his life and business fortunes. He said that Sarah was from "one of the best families in the Country & a Moderate

Portrait of John Carlyle, a prominent Scottish merchant and one of Alexandria's founders. *Courtesy of Carlyle House Historic Park, Alexandria, Virginia.*

fortune." Furthermore, Carlyle explained that the marriage "will enable me to Live Independent I am Apprehensive that Mr. Hicks & I Shall Not Agree Long together So am preparing to Settle with him."[16] In essence, Carlyle was declaring business independence. His marriage was a way to get there with his own import and export business.

Since Carlyle was also the son-in-law of Colonel Fairfax, George Washington and John Carlyle would have known each other by 1748. When Alexandria was founded in 1749, Carlyle bought two half-acre lots, 41 and 42, and was a trustee alongside Lawrence and Colonel Fairfax. Thereafter, he and his wife, Sarah, undertook construction of an exquisite Georgian-style sandstone mansion, which was completed by August 1, 1753. As John and Sarah moved into their new home, they also welcomed a baby boy named William. With much joy and anticipation, Carlyle wrote again to his brother, George, that it was a "fine beginning."[17]

While John Carlyle sought independence from William Hicks, it is clear from letters in the early 1750s that he was still doing business with Hicks and dependent on him for financing. As a result, when Virginia Lieutenant

Governor Dinwiddie approached Carlyle with an offer to be head of the commissary and paymaster of the Virginia Regiment, Carlyle was more than intrigued by the offer. With the new post, Carlyle was promised a £500 annual payment. Carlyle gladly accepted, although he did have apprehensions that the "post is attended with great trouble and fatigue."[18] Nevertheless, Carlyle was certain that the "profit makes up for the fatigue."[19]

Dinwiddie promoted Carlyle to captain. He also promoted George Washington to lieutenant colonel in the Virginia Regiment. After Washington returned from his 1753 mission, Dinwiddie called a series of emergency meetings of the Virginia House of Burgesses. He tried to rally Virginia and the other colonies to act against the French. Unfortunately for Dinwiddie, not everyone saw the French presence in the Ohio Country as an emergency. Recruiting was difficult. To entice volunteers, he promised land, specifically 200,000 acres of fertile land in the Ohio Country, for any volunteers who joined the newly formed Virginia Regiment.

Lieutenant Colonel Washington set up his headquarters in Alexandria. It was in Alexandria where he gathered new recruits for the Virginia Regiment and sought to instill discipline and basic military skills in them. Furthermore, he worked with John Carlyle to ensure that his soldiers were properly equipped and ready to march from Alexandria that spring. Both Washington and Carlyle encountered many obstacles in their new roles. In Alexandria, Washington worked for the first time to try to mold raw, inexperienced recruits into a professional fighting force. Where did George Washington get his military knowledge? Through the tutelage of his late brother Lawrence and his four years as a surveyor, Washington had acquired basic knowledge and skills that could translate into a soldier's life. However, in 1754, Washington gained his first experience in military leadership. It was the first time he commanded soldiers as part of a campaign.

When Washington left Alexandria in April 1754, his mission was no longer diplomatic; rather, it involved use of force if needed. As Washington marched with his regiment to the forks of the Ohio River, he soon learned that French forces had established a fort there called Fort Duquesne. With the mobilization of forces in a race to control the Ohio River Valley, bloodshed was inevitable. On May 28, 1754, the first shots of the French and Indian War were fired at Jumonville Glen. During this skirmish, a French scouting party encountered George Washington with members of his regiment and his Indian allies under Tanacharison, known as the Half-King. At one point, as the French were trying to surrender, the Half-King murdered the French commander, Lieutenant

Joseph Coulon de Villiers, Sieur de Jumonville. The Half-King scalped Lieutenant Jumonville. Washington watched in horror as the Frenchman was murdered in cold blood.

After learning about the bloody skirmish and death of Jumonville, French forces under the command of Captain Contrecœur mobilized a counterattack against Washington and his regiment. Washington had his soldiers set up an improvised fort in an open field known as the Great Meadows. The fort was called Fort Necessity. Since it was in an open field and surrounded by woods, it was a tactically poor position. French forces and their Indian allies exploited this military blunder. On July 3, 1754, French forces led by Louis Coulon de Villiers, who was the brother of Lieutenant Jumonville, surrounded the fort and fired a relentless volley of fire on the fort throughout the day. The casualties mounted, and one of the soldiers who witnessed the carnage firsthand was the regimental surgeon, Dr. James Craik.

Dr. Craik was born in 1730 in Dumfries, Scotland. He grew up in Scotland and received his medical training at the University of Edinburgh. After serving in the West Indies with the British army as a surgeon, Craik eventually made his way to Virginia. He first lived in Norfolk and later Winchester. When volunteers were called in 1754, Craik joined the Virginia Regiment in March and was a surgeon in the regiment. George Washington's first written record of Craik appears in his narrative of the expedition. On April 2, 1754, Washington reported departing from Alexandria with the following troop strength:

> *Two Companies of Foot, commanded by Captain Peter Hog, and Lieutenant Jacob Vambraam, five Subalterns, two Serjeants, six Corporals, one Drummer, and one Hundred and twenty Soldiers, one Surgeon, one Swedish Gentleman, who was a Volunteer, two Waggons, guarded by one Lieutenant, Serjeant, Corporal, and Twenty-five Soldiers.*[20]

The surgeon was Dr. Craik. Washington more than likely met Craik in March 1754. It was the start of a friendship that would last until the day Washington died on December 14, 1799. While Craik didn't claim Alexandria as home in 1754, he would eventually move to Alexandria to be closer to George Washington. Thus, Craik was George Washington's closest friend from Alexandria.

As bullets tore through the defenses of Fort Necessity on July 3, 1754, Craik was busy treating patients. As wounded soldiers wailed in pain and dead men were stacked to the side of the fort, Craik quickly realized how

Fort Necessity in western Pennsylvania, where George Washington commanded his first military engagement in 1754. *Courtesy of Mount Vernon.*

dire the situation was becoming. Craik provided counsel to Washington throughout his life, especially on matters of Washington's own health. Perhaps he counseled Washington on July 3, 1754, and influenced him to negotiate with the French.

With the fort surrounded, ammunition running low, and casualties mounting, Washington raised a white flag and began discussions with the French. Washington's interpreter, Jacob Van Braam, led the negotiations. Determining that the situation was untenable, Washington decided to abandon the fort.

Under a flag of truce, Washington and his regiment left the fort on July 4, 1754. While humbled by the loss of Fort Necessity, Washington displayed prudence and returned to Alexandria to replenish his men and equipment. Washington saw clearly that the French had the upper hand. They had gained the initial foothold in the Ohio Country. Getting rid of them would require a larger force with more manpower and equipment than he currently possessed. Washington was right, and the British decided to send more troops. A world war had erupted on the American frontier. Between the skirmish in Jumonville Glen and the battle at Fort Necessity, Washington and his Virginia Regiment had just fired the first shots of the French and Indian War.

# Chapter 4

# BRADDOCK'S CAMPAIGN

In March 1755, Major General Edward Braddock arrived on a flotilla carrying two British army regiments of the Forty-Fourth and Forty-Eighth Foot. They arrived in Alexandria with a total force of around 1,600 soldiers. The sudden influx of soldiers transformed the town. In the twenty-first century, it would be the equivalent of at least 500,000 people arriving in Alexandria overnight. The size of Braddock's army created enormous strain on a small, emerging port town. Any boon to the shops and taverns was quickly eclipsed by the disruption of a massive army being mobilized for war.

One such person who felt the strain was the head of the commissary, John Carlyle, whose beautiful stone mansion became the command post for Braddock and his staff. Whatever Carlyle's initial enthusiasm for hosting an esteemed military figure quickly dissipated with the inconvenience of playing host to high-ranking British officers, who were worried less with niceties than the necessity of their mission. And their mission was clear: take their army from Alexandria across the Alleghany Mountains and destroy the French forces at Fort Duquesne.

General Braddock was determined to achieve what Washington and his Virginia Regiment could not accomplish in 1754. Despite Washington's losses, his reputation was not damaged. Indeed, Washington was invited to join Braddock's staff as a volunteer aide-de-camp. At the time, Washington aspired to receive a commission as an officer in the British army. Successful service under General Braddock might make that dream possible.

The Carlyle House in Old Town Alexandria, home of merchant John Carlyle and the headquarters of Major General Edward Braddock in 1755. *Photo by the author.*

Braddock's Campaign was one of the more consequential events in American history. What happened during the campaign set America on a path toward independence. It was one of the first times in which British regulars and colonials came into close contact. Colonial Americans chafed under the poor treatment of their British counterparts. John Carlyle sent a letter to his brother, George, that spoke to the feeling of being treated like a second-class citizen. He specifically stated that the British treated us as the "spawn of convicts."[21] Carlyle griped further, "They Used Us Like an Enemy Country & Took everything they wanted & paid Nothing, or Very little for it."[22] Finally, he assessed Braddock's character as being "very Indolent, Slave to his Passions, Women & Wine, As Great an Epicure as could be in his Eating, Tho' A brave Man."[23] Thus, from the pen of John Carlyle, we read about the early seeds of colonial resentment two decades before the American Revolution erupted in 1775.

Additionally, Braddock's frustrations were manifested in a lack of coordination and support from the colonies. This problem was exemplified at a "grand congress" that was held on April 14, 1755, at Carlyle's house in Alexandria. Braddock invited five royal governors from Virginia, Maryland, Pennsylvania, New York, and Massachusetts. Each governor represented the interests of the king rather than elected by their respective colonies. They spoke bluntly to Braddock about the colonies' lack of willingness to fund the campaign of their own volition. In turn, Braddock and the governors concluded that the colonists' hand must be forced by parliament. Braddock wrote a letter to British Secretary of State Thomas Robinson in which he concluded the "necessity… of some Tax being Laid throughout His Majesty's Dominions in North America." Braddock's suggestion was clear that the British parliament must tax the colonies. While this was not the only conversation about taxation of the colonies without their direct representation, it was a discussion at the highest levels. Furthermore, it is one of the clearest early examples of how the British recognized that financing the French and Indian War was going to require colonial support through taxation. However, it was not until after the war that the system would be formally implemented beginning in 1764 with the Sugar Act and then followed in 1765 with the Stamp Act.

Despite the colonies' financial reluctance, Braddock and his army set off from Alexandria in April 1755. Douglas Southall Freeman wrote that Alexandria had "felt immense pride" in hosting Braddock and the meeting of five governors. In a letter from Washington to his patron, Colonel Fairfax, Washington wrote, "Alexandria has been honourd with 5 Governours in Consultation A favorable presage I hope, not only of the success of [Braddock's] Expedition, but for the future greatness of this Town."[24]

But the high spirits were dashed by the difficult march ahead.[25] Braddock thought that the journey through the Alleghany Mountains was only fifteen miles and was shocked to learn that it was between sixty and seventy.[26] His army cut a path through the dense wilderness of America's frontier, creating roads from scratch. Soldiers collapsed in the heat with little food and water. They battled a grueling wilderness filled with bears and venomous snakes. The supply train sprawled for miles. The movement was slow, and it took more than two months for the army to get close to Fort Duquesne.

As the campaign was planned and launched from Alexandria, George Washington got a close look at how a professional general ran an army. For all his tactical faults and idiosyncrasies, Braddock had decades of experience as a professional military officer. George Washington was only twenty-three years old with two years of experience and no formal military training. As Braddock grew the army to more than two thousand soldiers, including American provincials, Washington observed how a large army was mobilized and administered.

Throughout the march to Fort Duquesne, Washington struggled with a severe bout of dysentery or "bloody flux." It incapacitated him, and Washington worried that he might miss the battle when it finally occurred. However, Braddock promised Washington that he would be brought forward when the attack began. Washington felt assured that when the British conquered Fort Duquesne, he would be part of the glorious victory and, hopefully, achieve a coveted commission as a British regular officer.

While George Washington was sick, Dr. James Craik attended to him. Dr. Craik's presence with Washington during the Braddock Campaign continued to solidify the foundation of a lifelong friendship that began at Fort Necessity. In the case of Braddock's Campaign, we have the first example of Dr. Craik personally caring for George Washington as he would continue to care for him until the last day of George Washington's life on December 14, 1799.

George Washington recovered in time for the battle. Unfortunately, that battle came earlier than Braddock and his army hoped it would. On July 9, 1755, Braddock's army crossed the Monongahela River. They were seven miles from their objective at Fort Duquesne. The French and their Indian allies found advantageous pieces of high ground and waited patiently for the British army to fall into a carefully laid trap. Shots rang out through the woods accompanied by the bloodcurdling war whoops of the Indians. Chaos and confusion broke throughout the ranks of Braddock's army. They were unaccustomed to a style of fighting on the western frontier in which dispersed units used trees for cover and concealment. On European battlefields, it was important to form ranks and mass firepower to accommodate for the inaccuracy of muskets. However, on the western frontier, forming massed ranks presented a larger target opportunity for French soldiers, Canadian militia, and dispersed Indian warriors.

Braddock's army sustained heavy casualties as the ambush closed around them. Braddock was shot multiple times. He had four horses shot from under him. George Washington led Braddock's forces in a retreat. He stepped into the confusion and performed admirably under fire. Furthermore, Virginia and colonial militia units performed bravely under fire as well. Washington witnessed the ineffectiveness of British regulars fighting in the wilderness. Washington saw a disconnect between British soldiers' actions and their reputation as a disciplined, professional force. This memory remained with him for years.

As the reality of defeat set in, Braddock lamented, "Who would have thought it?" The campaign that started in Alexandria culminated in the woods of western Pennsylvania in utter disaster. Throughout the confusion and bloodshed, Washington felt the whizz of bullets around him. He was shot at but never hit. He counted four bullet holes through his coat. Two horses had been shot from under him. To say that he demonstrated extraordinary courage under fire would be an understatement. He rode his way through a shooting gallery and learned on the fly how to execute one of the most difficult military tactics imaginable, namely a withdrawal of troops under fire.

Perhaps George Washington was lucky. Or maybe there was a higher power at work. During the American Revolution, Dr. Craik assured Washington's aides-de-camp that he could not be injured or killed in battle "because an Indian prophet claimed that Washington was protected by a spirit."[27] It certainly appeared that was true, as Washington emerged unscathed from what became known as the disaster at the Monongahela.

In terms of reputational damage, General Braddock was scapegoated posthumously. He died on July 13, 1755. Despite the enormous tactical failures that had strategic consequences, Washington learned the mechanics of how to build and administer a professional army. Washington tried his best to emulate what he learned over the next three years. While he never received a British officer's commission, he was promoted to colonel in the Virginia Regiment. With that promotion, he returned to Alexandria, where he and his fellow Alexandrians dealt with the consequences of Braddock's defeat. He would need to lean on Alexandria's manpower and resources more than ever. With the French and Indian victory in the summer of 1755, violence and bloodshed were unleashed on the Virginia frontier.

# Chapter 5

# CHALLENGES OF COMMAND

Living on the western frontier of Virginia was a tough, hardscrabble existence. European settlers came to Virginia seeking religious freedom and economic independence. The frontier offered a bright opportunity to settle on cheap and abundant land, build a home, raise a family, and achieve economic prosperity. With great opportunity came great risk. Threats of violence hung over the heads of every American settler. After Braddock's defeat, Indian raids increased in frequency and intensity, gripping settlers in a state of panic and fear. In his book *Crucible of War*, Fred Anderson writes, "With so few soldiers to protect it, the frontier simply collapsed."[28]

George Washington took command of the Virginia Regiment and was given the nearly impossible task of defending Virginia's three-hundred-mile frontier. Under Braddock, Washington had received professional training in how to administer an army; over the next three years, he would try to do it himself. In one of the lesser-examined periods of Washington's life, the three-year period from Braddock's defeat until the Forbes Campaign of 1758 was one of the most formative for Washington as an officer. It was a crash course in how to raise, train, and discipline an army. There were also lessons in how to deal with infighting and political intrigue. Washington continued to struggle with the military supply chain, which he needed to equip and sustain an army. All the challenges and frustrations that Washington would deal with as commander-in-chief during the American Revolution, he first experienced during the French and Indian War as colonel of the Virginia Regiment. Moreover, he experienced those challenges in Alexandria.

Without his friends in Alexandria, Washington would not have been able to make it through this time. In fact, several of the Alexandria merchants played important roles in Washington's military life from 1755 to 1758. There are two who are specifically worthy of attention. One of them was a merchant named John Kirkpatrick, who served as George Washington's official secretary but also assumed unofficial roles as an aide-de-camp and intelligence officer.

John Kirkpatrick was from Kirkcudbright, Scotland. His years of service were from 1755 to 1757. After briefly returning to Scotland in 1758, he returned to Alexandria and sold supplies to the Virginia Regiment. Over the next decade, his business interests included shipbuilding and importing rum and molasses from the West Indies, and he had a warehouse built along Alexandria's waterfront east of Water Street (now Lee Street). Kirkpatrick was approved as town trustee in July 1762 and served presumably until his death sometime before February 1770.[29]

In his role as George Washington's secretary, Kirkpatrick began a pattern of influential Alexandrians who acted as Washington's staff officers, aka his "military family" during the French and Indian War and again during the Revolutionary War. During the French and Indian War, Washington relied on Kirkpatrick's services as a staff officer to help him with army administration, communications, intelligence, diplomacy, and general advice. Since Kirkpatrick was with Washington from 1755 to 1757, he spent the bulk of the critical three-year period of service with George Washington.

Another Alexandrian who was influential to Washington was William Ramsay. As previously mentioned, Washington honored Ramsay with Masonic rites at his funeral in 1785. Ramsay was older than Washington, as he was born in 1716. Like many Alexandrians, he was born in Scotland and specifically came from the Galloway district in the Scottish Lowlands. He came to Virginia sometime in the early 1740s. His original home was in Dumfries, Virginia. The location where his house once stood is currently the Alexandria Visitor Center at the intersection of King and North Fairfax Street. While the house was rebuilt after a destructive fire in the 1940s, the original house was believed to have been disassembled in pieces in Dumfries, Virginia, barged up the Potomac River, and reassembled on the high bluff over Alexandria's shoreline.

Both Kirkpatrick and Ramsay provided a lift to Washington's spirits during a low moment for him in late 1756. After one year as commander of the Virginia Regiment, Washington was about to throw in the towel. The world breathed down his neck. The impossibility of his regiment's mission to secure the frontier was compounded by the negativity of the press, specifically a newspaper called the *Virginia-Centinel.* The *Virginia-Centinel* relentlessly criticized the nature and scope of Washington's service. It was enough to drive him to the point of resignation.

As he considered resigning, Washington turned to his Alexandria friends for counsel. He first sought the advice of John Kirkpatrick, whom Douglas Freeman described as a "most devoted friend."[30] George Washington's question was, "Would Kirkpatrick inquire of George's friends and ascertain what they would think of his resignation?" Kirkpatrick told Washington to ignore the *Virginia-Centinel* and continue to serve. "I would Overlook the Scurrility of the Centinell, Continue to Serve My Country with the usual Zeal."[31]

Additionally, Kirkpatrick informed William Ramsay that Washington was upset by the bad press from the *Centinel.* Ramsay was a "long time friend" and encouraged Washington to remain in his place and ignore the censure of the *Centinel.* Ramsay specifically told Washington to "[s]hew your contempt of the Scribler by your Silence, your watchfulness & care, & thereby disappoint him."[32]

Washington's willingness to resign his commission clashes with the image of him as a stoic, self-confident general crossing the Delaware River in 1776. But Washington was in his mid-twenties, and the pressure of his command would have broken most men. Nevertheless, it was a time in which Washington leaned on his friends for encouragement. Ramsay signed his letter to Washington as his "sincere friend."

Washington and Ramsay continued to support each other. One year later, in the summer of 1757, Ramsay was in dire financial straits. He wrote to Washington and confessed, "I have been extremely unfortunate in all my affairs, which has greatly embarrassed me."[33] Ramsay came to Washington hat in hand and asked him for a modest loan of "[t]wo hundred or £250." Washington gave him £150 across two payments.[34] It was enough to sustain him. One month later, on September 3, 1757, Ramsay wrote to Washington with good news. He had secured a government contract from Governor Dinwiddie.[35] In the contract, Ramsay agreed to supply the officers and soldiers of Frederick and Hampshire Counties with provisions that included salt, pork, flour, beef, and biscuits.[36] Ramsay was also responsible for the transportation of these provisions. For that mission, Dinwiddie explicitly tasked Washington to provide a "proper escort" for Ramsay's transportation.[37] Like John Carlyle, Ramsay's fortunes were transformed by business tied to the military supply chain during the French and Indian War.

Plaque honoring William Ramsay, Scottish merchant and founder of Alexandria, on the exterior of the visitor center. *Photo by the author.*

Ramsay and Washington worked with each other until the fall of 1758. At the end of that year, Washington finally retired from his service as commander of the Virginia Regiment. Ramsay and Washington remained close friends. During one of the lowest moments in Washington's military career, Ramsay's encouragement provides a clear manifestation of the importance of Washington's friends and growing network in Alexandria.

# Chapter 6

## A DIFFICULT SEASON

The year after the incident with the *Virginia-Centinel*, the British were no closer to winning the French and Indian War. Beyond Virginia, the French consolidated their strength on the western frontier. British attempts to launch campaigns against the French were unsuccessful. Meanwhile, the British suffered a major defeat at Fort William Henry. When the British surrendered the fort in August 1757, the retreat turned into a massacre. France continued to sanction the harassment of British settlements by their Indian allies. As a result, the Virginia colonists felt their backs to the wall and a sense of standing alone in their own defense.

The strategic situation continued to frustrate Washington's efforts to secure the western frontier. There were also internal divisions, notably in the authority of his commission relative to a Maryland captain named John Dagworthy. As if Washington's military problems were not hard enough, he was also dealing with a mild case of dysentery and was spending time in Alexandria settling the estate of his late brother Lawrence, which included the Mount Vernon property. Furthermore, Lawrence had property in Alexandria. In fact, the two Alexandria lots that Lawrence purchased, lots 51 and 52, would eventually be sold on May 20, 1760, to a carpenter named John Patterson for £150.[38]

Dealing with illness and the personal affairs of Lawrence was compounded by another devastating loss. On September 3, 1757, Colonel William Fairfax of Belvoir died. Douglas Freeman wrote that Colonel William Fairfax was "the man who had done more than any other single individual to counsel

Plaque on Prince Street honoring Colonel William Fairfax and his son George William Fairfax, influential members of the Fairfax family, whose vast landholdings shaped colonial Virginia. *Photo by the author.*

and advance young George Washington."[39] He had been a father figure to George. With Colonel Fairfax's death, George lost a man on whom he relied for "moral assistance" and "sound counsel."[40] Washington acknowledged his affection and gratitude to Colonel Fairfax in a letter to his brother John Augustine. Washington wrote the letter on May 28, 1755, when he served as volunteer aide-de-camp to General Braddock. The disaster at the Monongahela had not occurred yet, and Washington had reason to be optimistic. George Washington told his brother that he should visit the Fairfax family at Belvoir. He added his reason, "for to that Family I am under many obligation[s] particularly to the old Gentleman."[41]

Between the stress of command and loss of Colonel Fairfax, Washington's dysentery or bloody flux deteriorated his condition. By the end of October, he was stationed in Winchester and on the verge of death. His subordinates encouraged him to take a leave of absence, so he would not succumb to his illness. Washington did not want to suffer an early death like other members of his family. After all, his father, Augustine, and brother Lawrence had both died young.

To get healthy, Washington returned to Alexandria in November 1757 and stayed at the home of his friend John Carlyle.[42] Dr. Charles Green was the first doctor to treat Washington. Washington would not recover until 1758 after seeking treatment from additional doctors. Nevertheless, the first person Washington sought to help him was his friend and leading Alexandria merchant John Carlyle. Washington must have had a lot on his mind. His brother had been dead for five years, and now his mentor and surrogate father was gone. He was a bachelor with no bright prospects of marriage. Furthermore, he was four years into his military service, and the British chances of victory seemed to slip away every day. Despite the many setbacks that he faced in 1757, Washington could take solace in one thing. As he lay in bed in Carlyle's Georgian-style mansion, he knew that his friends in Alexandria would remain steadfastly by his side no matter the circumstances.

# Chapter 7

# A DRAMATIC TURNAROUND

## A Courtship Begins

In February 1758, George Washington turned twenty-six. It may have been one of the lower moments of his life, but things were about to turn around, starting with his health. He traveled to Williamsburg in early March. While he was in Williamsburg, he met with a prominent English-born doctor named John Amson around mid-March. When Washington consulted Amson, he feared the worst, perhaps tuberculosis like his brother. However, the diagnosis was promising. Washington had a cold. He would recover with time. In fact, Dr. Amson assured Washington that he was on the mend. This news alone was enough to improve Colonel Washington's health.

The trip to Williamsburg corresponded with another visit that Washington paid to a widow named Martha Dandridge Custis. Her husband, Daniel Parke Custis, had died in 1757. Martha was living at the home she and Daniel had shared that was called the "White House" in New Kent County. She was managing an extensive property, including tobacco farms and enslaved laborers who had been owned by her wealthy late husband. Martha was slightly older than George, as she was born on June 2, 1731, at her family's plantation Chestnut Grove in New Kent. Like George, she was also in a season of difficulty as she balanced raising two children with the management of a seventeen-thousand-acre plantation. But George and Martha fell in love with each other. The courtship began in the spring of 1758. It would not last long, as they were married by the following spring.

Young Martha Washington, who married George Washington in 1759. *Courtesy of Mount Vernon.*

With George's health improving and his courtship to Martha beginning, news arrived that a new campaign was underway under the command of General John Forbes. By April 2, 1758, Washington was on his way back to Winchester to resume his command of the Virginia Regiment. On his way, he passed through Alexandria for business "partly of a public and partly of a private nature."[43] Washington's French and Indian War experience frequently took him back and forth from Williamsburg to Alexandria and then to the frontier fort at Winchester. Williamsburg was the colonial capital where he received his marching orders. Alexandria was where he recruited, trained, and equipped the troops in his regiment. Winchester was the front lines and the main fort defending the western frontier. After beginning his courtship of Martha, George looked forward to opportunities to get back to Williamsburg, stopping by the White House to see her. This included a trip back to Williamsburg in late May 1758.

Plaque in New Kent County marking the birthplace of Martha Dandridge Custis Washington, the future first lady. *Photo by the author.*

## Mount Vernon's First Expansion

As Washington became serious about marrying Martha, his plans to enlarge Mount Vernon began to materialize. He had leased the property from Anne Fairfax Washington since 1754. Anne had remarried George Lee and moved away. Due to his military service, Washington could not personally manage the property and relied on multiple overseers. One of the first overseers was George Washington's younger brother, John Augustine (Jack) Washington, who managed the property during the Braddock Campaign. After Jack, Humphrey Knight became the overseer in 1757 and managed the property until his death in the fall of 1758. It was Humphrey Knight who managed the property during the first phase of the expansion of Washington's mansion house.

While Knight was an overseer for the first part of the expansion, Washington hired a carpenter named John Patterson from Alexandria. Washington knew Patterson and had seen his work in Alexandria. Patterson was the carpenter who made repairs to the Fairfax County Courthouse, which was in Alexandria. Washington was impressed with Patterson's work and hired him in 1758. In 1760, as the first phase of the house expansion was completed, Patterson bought the two Alexandria lots that had been owned by Lawrence. John Patterson died in 1765. His wife, Susanna Patterson, eventually sold the lots to John Fitzgerald, who was a friend of George Washington and an aide-de-camp to him during the Revolutionary War.

The expansion of Mount Vernon included second-floor and third-floor "garret" rooms, which served as spare bedrooms. As Mount Vernon was being raised to three floors, Patterson wrote a letter to Washington on June 17, 1758, telling him, "I shall take the roof off the house."[44] Washington also expanded the first floor with the addition of "closets," which extended the north and south end of the mansion.

Due to his return to service, George Washington could not personally inspect the work at Mount Vernon. His letters to Patterson were frequently delayed. Furthermore, due to Humphrey Knight's declining health and death, Washington also enlisted the help of his friend and Alexandria trustee George William Fairfax, son of Colonel Fairfax. Washington and George William had been friends since their first survey expedition in 1748. George William Fairfax personally inspected the work at Mount Vernon on Washington's behalf. In fact, Fairfax specifically told Washington that he went to "spur Patterson on" with respect to the work on the expansion.[45] Fairfax offered Washington assurance that the work was progressing despite the delays in communication.

With a reliable carpenter from Alexandria and his friend George William Fairfax inspecting the project, Washington knew that the job would get done right. This allowed him to focus on the military campaign led by General Forbes. It had been more than three years since the Monongahela disaster under General Braddock. However, Forbes proved to be a much more skilled general.

## Victory Under General Forbes

The year 1758 was a turnaround both for the British and George Washington. British Secretary of State William Pitt implemented new policies that improved relations between Britain and America. Pitt's policies included shorter-term enlistments and higher pay for colonial volunteers. In April 1758, the Virginia House of Burgesses passed a law authorizing the creation of a new regiment and an expansion of the existing one that Washington led. The two Virginia Regiments numbered 1,850 total. The policy shift under Pitt dramatically improved Virginia's military recruitment and retention.

Thus, Washington commanded nearly one thousand soldiers under General Forbes. Despite Washington's objections to Forbes's line of attack against Fort Duquesne, Washington learned a lot from Forbes. In fact, Douglas Freeman writes, "Washington could not have found in America a better instructor in the art of army administration." Washington worked directly under two generals, Braddock and Forbes. These two generals showed Washington how to capably administer and run a professional army. As it turned out, Forbes was right about the best line of attack. Unlike Braddock, he was patient and thorough. He worked with "courage" and "cheer."

In the end, the Forbes Campaign was a success. The French abandoned Fort Duquesne in late 1758. It was one of a string of victories that led to the British finally defeating the French and signing a treaty with them in 1763. For Washington, the Fall of Fort Duquesne in 1758 closed the chapter on his service during the French and Indian War. For five years, he had fought for the British interest in the Ohio River Valley. He was ready to retire and settle down to his private life at Mount Vernon. Not only was his property growing with the expansion of the house, but he was about to grow his family as well. As 1759 approached, Washington prepared to make the familiar trip through Alexandria to Williamsburg. When he returned to Alexandria in the spring of 1759, he would return a married man.

# Chapter 8

# WASHINGTON AND THE ALEXANDRIA MERCHANTS

When Washington retired from the Virginia Regiment in December 1758, he was not returning to a quiet life of leisure. His home and farms at Mount Vernon needed work. He was determined to transition his energy as a military officer into success as a plantation manager. George Washington moved his new family to Mount Vernon in the spring of 1759 and shifted his focus to building Mount Vernon into a successful commercial enterprise.

To make Mount Vernon successful, Washington would rely heavily on friends in Alexandria who composed the town's vibrant merchant and business class. Alexandria was a decade old in 1759. Like George Washington, the town of Alexandria had been transformed by the French and Indian War. Washington had developed strong ties to John Carlyle and William Ramsay throughout the war, and now he looked to them for commercial rather than military support.

Through marriage, hard work, partnerships, and service as head of the commissary, John Carlyle was eventually able to reduce his dependence on William Hicks. In fact, Carlyle had established several business partnerships with fellow merchants in Alexandria. One of those partners was a merchant named John Dalton. Dalton was a second-generation American. His father settled in Gloucester, Virginia, in the late 1600s. Dalton was born on September 2, 1722. In 1744, Dalton moved to the small tobacco trading post north of Great Hunting Creek that would become Alexandria five years later.[46] In 1744, John Dalton went into business with John Carlyle.

The John Dalton House in Old Town Alexandria. Dalton served in the French and Indian War and conducted business with George Washington. *Photo by the author.*

The firm Carlyle & Dalton was one of the most prominent of Alexandria's early businesses. Carlyle & Dalton exported crops like tobacco and imported goods from the West Indies and Europe. As their business grew, they helped loosen the monopoly that London merchants and consigners of tobacco had over the American planters like George Washington.[47] Indeed, the partnership, which operated from 1744 until Dalton's death in 1777 was essential for Washington.

When Alexandria was founded on July 13, 1749, Dalton bought lots 37 and 36. In fact, lot 37 was the first of eighty-four half-acre lots sold. After Dalton's purchase of lot 37, he built a home that still stands to this day. He also built a brick building that later became a popular tavern after Dalton's death in 1777. The location is on the northeast corner of North Fairfax and Cameron Streets.[48] On February 22, 1750, Dalton became an Alexandria town trustee. He was directly in Washington's circle of influence and spent time with Washington's brothers and fellow trustees, Lawrence and Augustine Jr. Dalton fought alongside George Washington during the French and Indian War. Dalton was a captain in the Fairfax Militia and served on the frontier during the chaos that followed the Braddock Campaign.[49]

In the 1760s, Washington began to conduct more business with the firm Carlyle & Dalton. In 1761, Washington's sister-in-law, Anne Fairfax, died and left behind no children. Washington, who had been leasing Mount Vernon, inherited the property after the death of Anne. During the early 1760s, Washington thought of new products at Mount Vernon and ways to shift from dependence on tobacco. Moving from tobacco made Washington less reliant on British consigners like Robert Cary & Company.

Washington was frustrated with the consignment system. Under this system, Virginia farmers sent their tobacco to British consigners, who would hold their tobacco in warehouses and sell it at market prices. At the same time, the Virginia planters sent their British contacts a list of items to purchase. As the tobacco was sold, orders for other goods, including luxury items and household goods, were fulfilled. In many cases, planters were extended generous lines of credit and, thus, went into debt. This happened if the tobacco market rates were lower than expected while the items purchased exceeded the income from tobacco. Washington was frequently upset with how much income he received from the sale of his tobacco.

George Washington's financial records indicate that he did business with the firm Carlyle & Dalton from 1760 until 1769.[50] In one specific example from April 1760, Washington recorded, "Brought down 9 Hogsheads of Tobo. to go to the Inspection at Hunting [Creek Warehouse] in a flat which I borrowed (or I rather suppose hired) from Messrs. Carlyle and Dalton—which. Flat brought. down 4 Barrels of Corn—being part of Eight that I was to have had of William Garner at the rate of 9/. pr. Barl. to be paid in Pistoles or Dollars."[51] We see how Washington relied on Carlyle & Dalton for transportation and inspection of his tobacco in Alexandria. Concurrently, the note about corn also indicates that Washington was experimenting with other crops like corn.

John Carlyle was not only a business partner with John Dalton but also with a merchant named Robert Adam. Adam was a man of influence in Alexandria both as a merchant and in the social fabric of Alexandria as a Freemason. Throughout his life in Alexandria, Adam operated a store, gristmill, tannery, iron foundry, and bakery.[52] He partnered with John Carlyle to form the firm Carlyle & Adam.

Originally, Alexandria merchants had helped Washington inspect tobacco from Mount Vernon before exporting it in hogsheads to Europe. However, Alexandria merchant firms promised Washington an even greater opportunity. They provided an expanded market for products that he was experimenting with on his farms at Mount Vernon. The most promising of these products included different types of wheat. Wheat had potential to be a better crop than tobacco. Tobacco wore out the soil and was more labor intensive, with enslaved labor harvesting the crops. Wheat was more sustainable and required less physical labor. So, Washington gradually increased Mount Vernon's output of wheat. In 1763, Washington agreed to a seven-year contract with Carlyle & Adam in which the firm bought Washington's wheat and exported it from Alexandria.

Several years into the contract, Washington cut back on his tobacco production significantly. By 1767, he was no longer cultivating tobacco at Mount Vernon. Instead, Washington farmed wheat and corn. According to biographer Ron Chernow, Washington also "tested hemp, flax, and sixty different crops." His experiments with different crops allowed him to diversify his portfolio of products. As he tested his crops, wheat emerged as the primary replacement for tobacco. Chernow writes that it became Washington's "main cash crop, which he could sell locally in Alexandria."[53] Washington's shift to wheat went hand in hand with Alexandria shifting from being a port town where tobacco was the major export to wheat becoming the dominant export by 1800.

The George Gilpin House in Old Town Alexandria, home of the Revolutionary War officer and friend of George Washington's; Gilpin also served as a pallbearer at Washington's funeral. *Photo by the author.*

As Washington's production of wheat, corn, and other crops increased in the 1760s, he decided to build a new gristmill in 1769. The gristmill allowed him to take his wheat and grind it into fine flour. His corn was turned into cornmeal. Washington found a market for his flour also in Alexandria. This brought Washington into contact with other prominent merchants, including John Fitzgerald and George Gilpin. Both men served with George Washington during the Revolutionary War. After the war, Gilpin and Fitzgerald returned to their business as Alexandria merchants and worked with George Washington on new ventures like the Potomac Company.

John Fitzgerald was originally from Ireland and settled in Alexandria in 1769. He went into business with a man named Valentine Peers, and together they opened a firm called Fitzgerald and Peers. Fitzgerald was unique as one of the few Irish Catholics not only in Alexandria but also in northern Virginia. Together, Fitzgerald and Peers exported wheat and later flour. Fitzgerald eventually built a large warehouse and imported goods from around the world, which he sold in Alexandria.

George Gilpin was born in Cecil County, Maryland. He was a wheat and flour merchant in Alexandria and later became Alexandria's inspector of flour. Like George Washington, he was industrious and entrepreneurial. He was also a member of Christ Church and served on the vestry. After Washington's death, Gilpin, who was a member of Masonic Lodge No. 22, was a pallbearer to George Washington and performed Masonic rites at his funeral on December 18, 1799.

Finally, while Washington diversified his business with new crops, he also looked for opportunities in the Potomac River. As Mount Vernon was situated on the Potomac River, Washington was able to fish "shad, herring, bass, carp, sturgeon," which were "in great abundance." Chernow writes that "by 1772 Mount Vernon's fishery netted almost a million herring a year." Like wheat, Alexandria was where he found a market for his fish, turning again to the firm of Carlyle & Adam. Washington's ledgers record the number of fish that he delivered to Carlyle & Adam's firm, including one delivery of 679,200 herring and 7,760 shad. Additionally, the hemp that Washington grew was used to build nets for fishing, which manifests the ways in which Washington was building Mount Vernon into a self-sustaining enterprise.

After the French and Indian War, Washington worked hard and found innovative ways to grow his business at Mount Vernon. His success would not have been possible without a market of willing buyers for his most valuable products of wheat and fish. Washington found that market in Alexandria. Furthermore, Alexandrians found valuable products from Mount Vernon. Washington and the Alexandria merchants worked mutually for each other's benefit. In doing so, they were becoming economically less dependent on Great Britain. At the same time, Britain was seeking to impose new taxes and regulations on the American colonists. As we will see, the trend of colonial financial independence had larger ramifications as it would also accelerate a desire for political independence.

# Chapter 9

# WASHINGTON BECOMES AN ALEXANDRIA TRUSTEE

While Washington's service ended in 1758, the French and Indian War formally concluded with the Treaty of Paris in 1763. With the end of hostilities, the frontier was pacified without the French threat. Despite a British government-imposed proclamation line to halt westward expansion across the Appalachian Mountains, American colonists continued settling farther west.

Many of the American colonists chafed at the proclamation line and perceived high-handedness of Britain's concession to Indian tribes. George Washington and other French and Indian War veterans had been promised land as compensation for their service. They were determined to acquire what had been promised specifically by Governor Dinwiddie in 1754.

As settlers pushed west in defiance of British policy, Alexandria also expanded west through authorization from the Virginia House of Burgesses in November 1762.[54] In May 1763, a total of fifty-eight half-acre lots were auctioned for sale. George Washington acquired two of these lots. One of them was on the corner of Cameron and North Pitt Streets. The other was located at the corner of Prince and South Pitt Streets. Washington bought his two lots and recorded the transaction in 1764. He paid a total of £48 and 10s for both lots. In 2025, the price would be approximately $15,000. It demonstrated Washington's faith in the prospects of Alexandria and the continued growth of the town into what was destined to become a bustling port city. Furthermore, it was the sale of Washington's wheat by Carlyle

& Dalton that provided him with the money to buy his lots. In a letter dated February 15, 1767, Washington wrote about the transaction as follows: "In April 1764 I delivered the Wheat, in Septr following I recd my Bond which I passd for the purchase of some Lotts in Alexandria as payment."[55]

Lot 118 at the corner of Cameron and Pitt Streets was the lot where Washington made plans to have a house built. It should not be surprising that he chose Cameron Street. Historically, Cameron Street was the main street in Alexandria, as it was in the center of seven original streets running east–west. The name derived from Lord Fairfax, Sixth Baron of Cameron.

The construction of Washington's townhouse on Lot 118 began in 1769 by two Alexandria builders. Unlike the first auction in 1749, there was no stipulation that landowners had to build within two years. Washington paid £30 and 19s to Edward Rigdon, who was a local joiner. He paid £59 and 16s to Richard Leake, who at one time kept an ordinary (i.e., a tavern) in Alexandria. On September 28, 1769, Washington recorded, "I rid to Alexandria to see how my House went on."[56] The total cost to build his modest townhouse would be the equivalent price of $27,500 in 2025. Thus, the total sum of Washington's investments in Alexandria property prior to 1771 was the equivalent of about $42,000 in 2025.[57]

While Washington had a house on Lot 118, the half-acre property on Lot 112 at the intersection of South Pitt and Prince Streets remained "unimproved" until the end of his life. However, Washington had the property "laid off into proper sized lots for building on—three or 4 of which are let on ground Rent—forever—at three dollars a foot on the Street."[58] By 1799, Washington made plans to have it developed and available for rent. But Washington died before the completion of this plan.

Nevertheless, the completion of the first house was done in roughly two years. It was not a fancy house, rather a simple Colonial clapboard-style home. By 1771, Washington could use it as he did when he traveled to court in Alexandria on August 20, 1771, and recorded the following in his diary: "20. Went up to Court again and lodgd in my own House."[59] Since George

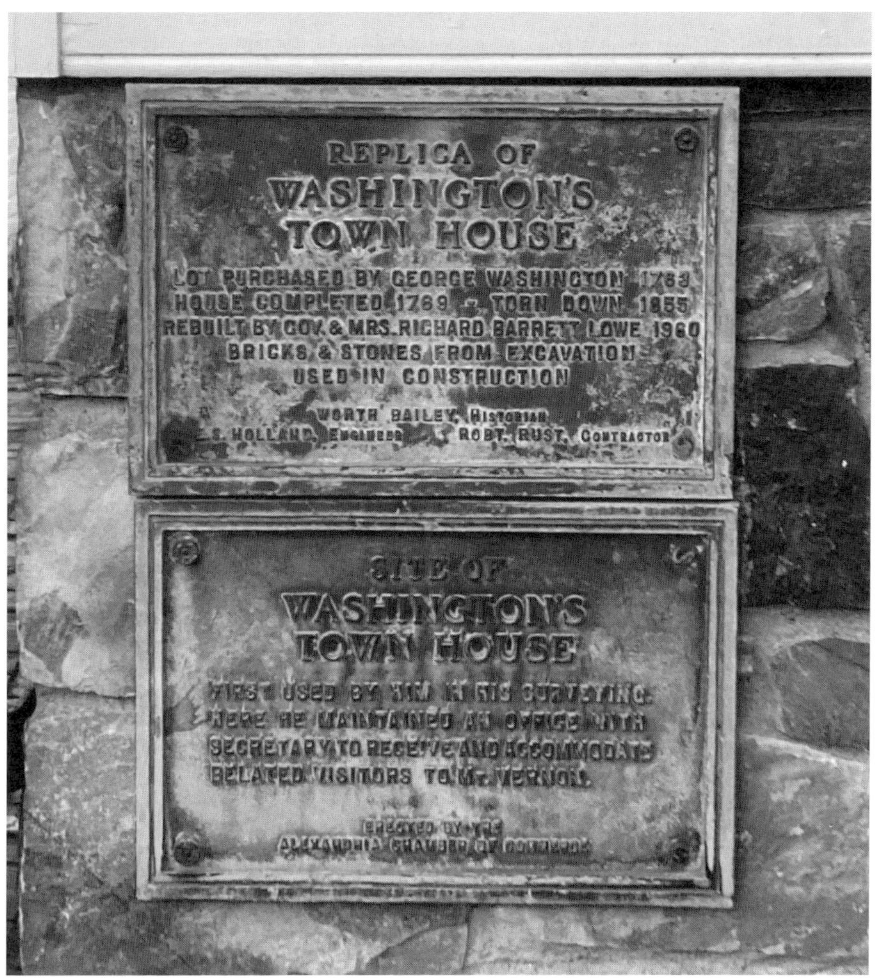


*Opposite*: George Washington's townhouse in Old Town Alexandria, built in 1769. Washington stayed here during visits to the city and later rented the property. *Photo by the author.*

*Above*: Plaque on the replica townhouse in Alexandria marking the site of George Washington's 1769 residence. *Photo by the author.*

Washington served as a justice of the peace for Fairfax County, he made frequent visits to the Fairfax County Courthouse in Alexandria and would stay over at his townhouse.[60]

While there are multiple references to Washington staying at his own house, records show that the home was used by family and rented to friends and neighbors. Since Washington spent eight years away as commander-in-chief (1775–83) and then eight years away as president (1789–97), it is not surprising that he would have wanted to keep the property occupied. In fact, one of Washington's letters to his nephew, Bushrod, indicated that an Alexandria physician, Dr. William Brown, lived in the townhouse. In the letter dated November 25, 1788, Washington wrote to tell Bushrod, "You could accommodate yourself in my small house there (the one in which Doctr Brown formerly lived)."[61] Another good example of Washington making his house available for rent comes from a letter to John Fitzgerald, William Herbert, and George Gilpin. In the letter, dated November 22, 1797, Washington told his friends that he agreed to rent his house for three years to Colonel Philip Marsteller. However, Washington confessed that he did not know what the rent should be and so he "would leave it to you three Gentlemen…to say what it should be."[62]

Since George Washington bought two lots in Alexandria, he qualified to become a trustee to the town of Alexandria. The trustee system existed prior to Alexandria's formal incorporation in 1779. It was the government of the city. It functioned as an oligarchy, but a better modern-day analogy could also be the board of a homeowner's association. The trustees were a coalition of property owners that managed the affairs of the town collectively. When Alexandria became a city, the form of government became more democratic with a council and elected mayor.

When George Washington joined the ranks of Alexandria trustees, he was thirty-one years old. It was the same age that his brother Lawrence became a trustee to Alexandria in 1749. George Washington was already close to Alexandria, but with the purchase of his land and inclusion as a trustee, he was fully enmeshed in the fabric of Alexandria. With Washington's growing financial prosperity and strong reputation, he was able to support the town as much as the town supported him. His selection as trustee foreshadowed another political event in 1765 that strengthened Washington's connection with Alexandria.

## Chapter 10

# WASHINGTON REPRESENTS ALEXANDRIA IN THE HOUSE OF BURGESSES

George Washington was first elected to the Virginia House of Burgesses in 1758. He was a burgess for Frederick County, which was in western Virginia. In fact, Douglas Freeman writes that Washington's friends in Alexandria, John Carlyle and George William Fairfax, campaigned on his behalf by mobilizing their land tenants to vote for him. With the electioneering of his Alexandria friends and generous quantities of alcohol, Washington was able to win the poll. Thus, the father of America first held elected office at age twenty-six and represented a county that he did not even live in, although he did own property there.

His experience in the House of Burgesses provided him with an early political education. He saw how laws were made in Williamsburg. In fact, George Washington attended a session of the 1762 House of Burgesses when one of the acts that was passed authorized the expansion of Alexandria, which formally occurred in 1763.

In 1765, a seat in the House of Burgesses opened for Fairfax County. George Johnston, who served from 1758 to 1765, struggled with health issues and declined to stand for reelection. Washington saw an opportunity to switch seats. He decided to enter the poll for Fairfax County rather than Frederick County.

Washington and Johnston had known each other for several years. Johnston was a prominent lawyer in Alexandria and a town trustee. Washington relied on his legal services on multiple occasions. In the last year of Johnston's tenure in the House of Burgesses, tensions escalated over the British Stamp

The George Johnston House in Old Town Alexandria, home of George Johnston, lawyer to George Washington and member of the Virginia House of Burgesses. Johnston died in 1766, and Washington took his seat in the House of Burgesses. *Photo by the author.*

Act. The Stamp Act was introduced by British Parliament to pay for high debts from the very expensive French and Indian War. It was one of the most significant early efforts to shift portions of the cost burden onto the American colonists. The Stamp Act caused a political upheaval. In Virginia, the act's primary opponent was a young lawyer from Hanover County named Patrick Henry. Henry introduced resolutions against the Stamp Act in May 1765. However, he was assisted by a lawyer from Alexandria. George Johnston's important contribution on the road to American independence was his standing up in support of Henry's Stamp Act Resolution.

In response to the House of Burgesses voting in favor of Patrick Henry's Stamp Act Resolution, Virginia's Royal Governor Francis Fauquier dissolved the House of Burgesses on June 1, 1765.[63] The political opposition to the Stamp Act was the opening salvo in a string of protests that took place over the next decade until George Washington was called to take command of a new American army that fought for American independence. It was also the inevitable consequence of a meeting that had occurred almost ten years prior at John Carlyle's house in Alexandria. The Alexandria Conference, which met prior to

Braddock's Campaign, foreshadowed the taxes that Britain attempted to implement on its colonial subjects. George Johnston's final act as a burgess representing Alexandria was a defiant one. His successor, George Washington, proved to be equally defiant.

The House of Burgesses election took place on July 16, 1765. It was an electoral victory for George Washington, who won 201 votes out of 256 total. Unlike his two elections to presidency, it was not a unanimous decision. Nevertheless, Washington's political base included his strong Alexandria network. Among those Alexandrians who voted for George Washington were prominent merchants like John Carlyle and John Dalton. Descendants of John Alexander, Robert and Philip, also voted for Washington. George William Fairfax voted for his friend, as did George Johnston and George Mason.

Over the next ten years, George Washington served as the Fairfax County representative in the Virginia House of Burgesses. Since Alexandria was then part of Fairfax County and was the seat of the county courthouse, George Washington served on behalf of Alexandria. As both a trustee and member of the House of Burgesses, George Washington represented Alexandria's political interests both locally and statewide. From the beginning of his political career in 1758, Washington's friends in Alexandria campaigned and voted for him. As he grew in stature as a trustee to Alexandria, his political support continued to enlarge. As a result, he had a strong political base in Alexandria by 1765. Washington continued to build on that political base over the next ten years until he left for the Second Continental Congress in 1775. In that year, he would be serving all of America as commander-in-chief. Furthermore, he would deal with politicians of all kinds from all thirteen states. However, Washington's political education, representing Alexandria in the Virginia House of Burgesses, was a firm foundation that helped him prepare for the politics of the American Revolution.

# Chapter 11

# WASHINGTON AND THE CHURCH IN ALEXANDRIA

As colonial Virginia was an English colony, the established church was the Church of England. To this day, Virginia still has many historic churches affiliated with the Episcopal Diocese that were part of the Church of England. In Alexandria, Christ Church Episcopal was formerly part of the Church of England and was included in Fairfax Parish. Since George Washington's Mount Vernon property fell within Fairfax Parish, Washington was a parishioner and, thus, a member of the church. He attended services at what he referred to as the "Alexandria church" or the "church in Alexandria" in Fairfax Parish.

However, Mount Vernon overlapped with a second parish. So, Washington was also a parishioner of Truro Parish and attended services at Pohick Church. Today, Pohick Episcopal Church is in Lorton, Virginia, near the U.S. Army base Fort Belvoir (named after Belvoir Manor). The Alexandria Church is now known as Christ Church Episcopal.* Both churches are still active houses of worship. They are part of the Episcopal Diocese of Virginia. However, they can be described as "Anglican" in that their roots are in the Church of England.

A parish was a geographic area that was established as population growth required a church for religious and civic order. In colonial Virginia, church and state were not separated. Parishioners were required to support the

* In Washington's life, the name "Christ Church" was not used. Washington referred to the church as the "Alexandria church" or "church in Alexandria." However, for simplicity, we will refer to Washington's attendance at Christ Church throughout the book.

Christ Church in Alexandria, built between 1767 and 1773 as part of the Church of England's Fairfax Parish. *Photo by the author.*

church both in terms of their time and resources. As Fairfax County grew in population, Fairfax Parish was created to administer the spiritual and moral needs of the people. Fairfax Parish was formally established in 1765. Two churches were set up in the parish. One was in Alexandria, and the other was located at a small town near the falls of the Potomac River and became known as "Falls Church."

In Alexandria, there was a chapel that existed outside the town limits in a small, modest building. It was known as the "chapel of ease." However, with the growth of the town, plans were eventually made to build a larger and enduring church that could house hundreds of faithful parishioners.

George Washington was elected to the vestry of both Fairfax Parish and Truro Parish. As a sign of his growing influence, the selection of Washington to the vestry was in the same year as his election to represent Fairfax County in the Virginia House of Burgesses. Like his membership in the House of Burgesses, Washington's appointment to the vestry solidified his prominent position in society. He was thirty-three years old and was now one of Alexandria and northern Virginia's most influential leaders.

It is worth noting that he was elected to the vestry in both Fairfax and Truro. However, he served on the vestry of Truro Parish. There is no record of Washington's service on the Fairfax Parish vestry after his election in 1765. Nevertheless, he was still elected to the Fairfax vestry, which demonstrates the reverence and respect that many people, including parishioners in Alexandria, had for George Washington.

To this day, an Episcopal church still has a vestry. The vestry is responsible for church governance in administrative matters rather than spiritual ones. They are typically laymen who make important decisions about the operations of the church, particularly as it pertains to financial stewardship of the church's resources. However, in colonial Virginia, the

Christ Church in Alexandria, completed in 1773. George Washington attended services here before departing to serve as commander-in-chief of the Continental army. *Photo by the author.*

parish vestry took on many functions that would be considered like social services today. While churches are still involved in charitable outreach, the vestry made very specific decisions to dedicate church resources to the care of the poor, orphans, and widows. As a result, Washington's election to the vestry meant that his fellow citizens trusted him in the important duty of making sure all parishioners, including the most downtrodden, received proper care and support.

Additional decisions made by the vestry included setting the salary of the rector and dedicating funds to the improvement of the church. As a result, the Fairfax vestry approved the decision to have an entirely new church built in Alexandria. Plans were put in motion as early as 1766. The church architect was a "master builder and member of Fairfax parish" named James Wren. Construction commenced in 1767. The first builder to implement Wren's design was a man named James Parsons. The vestry paid Parsons £600 sterling for his work. However, Parsons left the work incomplete in 1772. Without a finished product, the vestry approached John Carlyle to complete the construction. Carlyle was able to do so based on an agreed contract of £220 sterling.

By February 1773, the vestry was ready to receive an impressive church that became known as the "church in the woods." This name alludes to the fact that the original location of the church was outside the town limits of Alexandria. The exterior of the church remains as visually stunning today as it did in 1773. It is a brick sanctuary laid in Flemish bond with decorative quoins on the corners that were built from locally sourced Aquia sandstone. John Carlyle's house, built from Aquia sandstone, also includes quoins.

The entrance to the church is on the west side of the church by design. On the east side of the church is the chancel. Flanking the chancel are two notable panels. As one faces the chancel, the panel to the right was hand-painted with the Ten Commandments. Painted on the left side of the chancel is the Lord's Prayer, the Apostles' Creed, and the Golden Rule. The panels were hand-painted in 1773 and have been unaltered to this day. There is little direct sunlight on them. According to church history, the panels were painted on a white backdrop. Thus, the darker golden hue is a product of aging. The visual of the gold panels presents a striking contrast with the simple, white purity of the repainted walls. Visitors and churchgoers marvel at how each panel seems to symbolize the endurance of God's law (right panel) fulfilled by His son Jesus Christ (left panel).

As a member of Fairfax Parish, George Washington had a direct interest in the affairs of the church along with its growth and development. When the church contracted John Carlyle to finish the construction in 1772, the vestry made plans to raise funds to pay Carlyle through the auction of ten box pews. When the church was completed in 1773, it contained thirty-two box pews. Ten of these pews were sold to raise £220 to pay John Carlyle.

George Washington committed to purchase a box pew. At some point, after promising to sell the box pews, the vestry had a meeting in which they decided to scrap the sale of box pews and find another way of raising the money. George Washington was not happy when he heard about the new plan. He was so committed to owning a box pew that he wrote a letter of protest to his friend and vestryman John Dalton. Washington was upset because he had received word of a "scheme" to have his money refunded for the purchase of his box pew.[64]

When Dalton read Washington's letter, he must have understood that refunding the box pew payment was a bad idea. The vestry soon dropped the "scheme" of refunding the box pew money to each "subscriber." Instead, the vestry re-committed to selling the ten box pews as originally promised. Thus, Washington bought pew number five for a price of 36 pounds and 10 shillings, which is slightly under $9,000 in modern dollars.[65] To this day, people can still see and sit in George Washington's box pew.

George Washington's ownership of a box pew was no different than his election to the vestry or the House of Burgesses. It meant that he was a leader and respected person in Alexandria. Paying for a box pew was not done as a means of showing off wealth. It signified George Washington's support and commitment to the church and its teachings.

There has been extensive analysis about the personal faith of George Washington. There are a range of interpretations today as in Washington's lifetime. Some people think that he was pious, and some think he was not at all. However, what is indisputable is that Washington supported organized

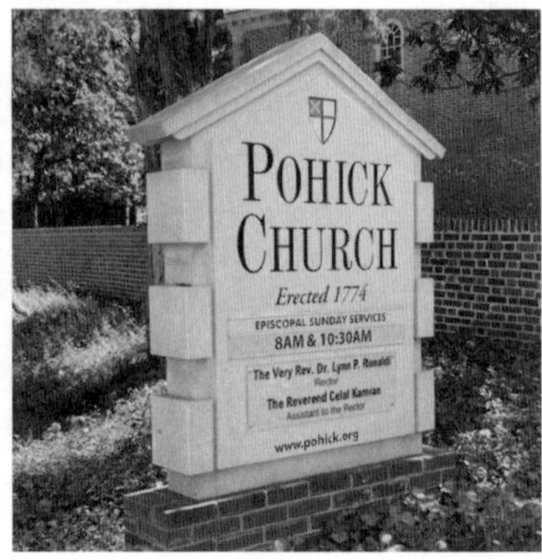


*Left*: George Washington's box pew at Christ Church in Alexandria, where he worshiped regularly with his family. *Photo by the author.*

*Right*: Pohick Church in Lorton, Virginia, constructed by 1774 as part of Truro Parish. Washington served as a vestryman here. *Photo by the author.*

religion and believed that it provided the backbone of moral teaching and cultivated civic virtue. Douglas Freeman summarizes Washington's religious mind as being instructed in "conduct rather than toward creed."[66] This belief would have been entirely consistent with the beliefs of his time even among those who embraced Enlightenment ideas about reason and rationality over faith and revelation.

George Washington regularly attended church in Alexandria. In fact, as we will see, George Washington attended services during tense moments, including as the American colonies mobilized toward war. However, this time the war would not be against the French to secure the Ohio Country for the British. It would rather be against the British to secure independence for America. In that war, Washington and his fellow parishioners would be fighting a war that ultimately led to severing the ties of the Alexandria church and other colonial Virginia churches with the Church of England. However, in the late 1760s, as the new church in Alexandria was being built, George Washington was still loyal to the king and the Church of England. Furthermore, he was dealing with many personal and professional issues for which he relied on his friends in Alexandria.

# Chapter 12

# WASHINGTON CALLS AN ALEXANDRIA DOCTOR

George Washington turned to Alexandria not only for his business interests but also for personal needs such as medical care. Many doctors from Alexandria became close friends with Washington, including Dr. James Craik and Dr. William Brown. However, there is a lesser-known doctor who was George Washington's family physician throughout the late 1760s and early 1770s.

Dr. William Rumney was born and received his medical education in England. He came to America during the French and Indian War and was a surgeon in the British army. After the war concluded in 1763, he moved to Alexandria and practiced medicine. Rumney was highly regarded, and as his reputation grew, George Washington sought his medical advice specifically for his family.

When George Washington married Martha, she had two children from her first marriage. Martha's daughter was Martha Parke Custis, known as "Patsy." Patsy was born in 1756. Martha's son was John Parke Custis, who was called "Jacky." Jacky was born in 1754. Since Patsy and Jacky's father, Daniel Parke Custis, died in 1757, neither child would have much memory of him. As a result, George Washington became like a father to both children as they lived at Mount Vernon.

Washington called on Rumney specifically for Patsy, who struggled with epileptic seizures from an early age. When Patsy was twelve years old, her condition became severe. According to biographer Ron Chernow, "In 1768 George and Martha were returning from Belvoir with twelve-year old Patsy when she suffered her first full-scale seizure."[67] It was this episode that brought Dr. Rumney from Alexandria to Mount Vernon on a regular basis starting in 1768. Washington's first record of spending time with Dr. William Rumney can be found in a diary entry dated January 3, 1768. In the entry, Washington simply noted, "At Home with Doctr. Rumney."[68]

To underscore how severe the seizures were, Rumney returned the following month on February 24, 1768. From Dr. Rumney's receipts, we know that he prescribed the girl "12 powders of unidentified composition," "a vial of Nervous Drops," and a "package of valerian."[69] Valerian is a flower native to Europe and Asia, and it has historically been considered a cure for epileptic spasms. In addition to valerian, on June 6, 1768, Rumney prescribed Patsy "a large Julep, probably a syrupy, nonalcoholic drink intended to soothe her nerves."[70]

Patsy's seizures continued into her teenage years. As the condition did not improve, Rumney experimented with other treatments, including "Best Bark," aka "Peruvian bark," which was from a plant in South America and was a popular medicine for epilepsy as well as malaria.[71] None of these treatments helped. Rumney continued to do the best he could and even sought second opinions. No one could find a cure for Patsy's epilepsy. The condition worsened. Chernow writes, "During one frightful period from June 29 to September 22, 1770, Patsy fell to the floor in convulsions no fewer than twenty-six times."[72]

The Stabler-Leadbeater Apothecary in Old Town Alexandria, established in 1792. The pharmacy served generations of Alexandrians, including George and Martha Washington. *Photo by the author.*

Finally, on June 19, 1773, Patsy Custis suffered her final epileptic seizure. It had been a little over five years since the Washingtons had first sought Rumney's assistance. Her death was not due to lack of effort on Rumney's part. As hard as he tried, Rumney could not cure Patsy. Neither could he stave off the grief and heartache that Patsy's death caused at Mount Vernon. However, Washington continued to hold the doctor in high regard as they saw each other in social settings. In fact, Rumney visited Mount Vernon frequently after Patsy's death.

One notable visit was on July 11, 1774, amid a fraught political moment in Virginia. The colony was quickly moving along with the rest of America toward an impasse with the British parliament. The start of the Revolutionary War was less than a year away. One week later, both Washington and Rumney would be in Alexandria to sign an important document that would lay the political foundation for American independence. Thus, Washington and Rumney's conversations were perhaps less about medicine and more about politics. Rumney would become an important part of Washington's network of American Patriots that supported the fight for American independence.

Like the merchants in Alexandria, Rumney was one of many Alexandrians who first knew Washington professionally, served with him in war, and then came to know him as a friend. During this period of Patsy's illness from 1768 to 1773, Washington relied on Alexandria's skilled doctors. At the same time, before the Revolutionary War began, Washington decided to take a bold risk in his business at Mount Vernon. As a result, he looked to Alexandria for another important professional service. As we will see, Washington needed a good lawyer.

# Chapter 13

# WASHINGTON SEEKS LEGAL ADVICE IN ALEXANDRIA

Washington's friends from Alexandria included veterans of the French and Indian War, merchants, doctors, members of his church, and lawyers. As Washington took possession of Mount Vernon and grew the property, he immediately ran into legal issues as he sought to expand his property and his business interests. One of the legal hurdles involved Washington's first expansion of Mount Vernon in December 1757. Washington acquired five hundred acres of land from Sampson Darrell for £350 but hit a roadblock when it was discovered that the land "was held under right of dower by Darrell's mother."[73] After the purchase, Washington wrote a letter to George Johnston on January 5, 1758, seeking his help.[74]

Johnston also advised Washington on a legal controversy involving a man named John Ballendine, who ran an ironworks on Occoquan Creek. Washington believed that Ballendine had defrauded him out of iron shipments. In short, Washington paid for the iron, but it was never delivered. Thus, Washington recorded in his diary on January 8, "Directed an Indictment to be formed by Mr. Johnston against [John] Ballendine for a fraud in some Iron he sold me."[75] Johnston's reply to Washington showed that he thought Ballendine was a cheater with "prodigious abilities in the art of being a Villain."[76] There had been prior suits brought against Ballendine, and Johnston advised Washington that it would be hard for him to recover his money. Washington wrote the money off as a loss.

When George Johnston became ill in 1765, Washington succeeded him as a member of the House of Burgesses, representing Alexandria. As discussed in a previous chapter, Johnston died in 1766. However, Washington maintained a connection to Johnston through his family. A smart, talented lawyer named Robert Hanson Harrison was George Johnston's son-in-law. Harrison was originally from Maryland. However, he moved to Alexandria and opened a legal practice around 1770. Like his father-in-law, Harrison also provided legal services to George Washington. And like Johnston's legal advice, Harrison counseled Washington on property disputes, business issues, or a combination of the two.

In 1769, George Washington saw a prime piece of real estate owned by his neighbor Captain John Posey. Posey had accumulated significant debts and struggled with personal issues, including drunkenness. However, Posey possessed two hundred acres of pristine riverfront land. Some of Posey's debts were owed directly to Washington. Harrison advised Washington on how to successfully pursue a legal strategy to gain title to Posey's land. It was a tough battle with an obstinate neighbor. But on October 7, 1769, Washington informed Harrison of good news. While at dinner, Washington wrote, "[Posey] came here…perfectly Sober and proposed of his own voluntary motion to sell his Estate finding it in vain to struggle any longer against the Torrent of Debt that oppresses him."[77]

Washington's successful acquisition of land adjacent to Mount Vernon expanded the total property size from 2,500 acres to 8,000 acres. With the property came exciting opportunities, and Washington had ambitions to build a new gristmill. This was the inevitable consequence of his wheat and corn production. The market for wheat corresponded with the market for flour, which Washington found in Alexandria. A new gristmill would allow him to capitalize on that market opportunity.

However, like so many of Washington's business plans, legal issues followed. Washington sought Harrison's legal advice on the right to use water (aka "riparian rights") on Dogue Run Creek to power his gristmill. Since the water from the creek benefited multiple property owners with land adjacent to the creek, water being diverted from the creek to Washington's mill posed a problem and opened him up to potential lawsuits. In this case, Harrison told Washington that he needed to get permission from the property owners, or they would likely sue him.

George Washington decided that he would go beyond merely getting permission. In fact, he would get the land! This led Washington into two separate negotiations with Valinda Wade and William Barry over land known as the Wade-Barry tract. The acquisition of Valinda Wade's property was completed with a deed of sale dated December 18, 1770. Washington acquired 193 acres for £175.[78]

However, acquiring William Barry's land was more difficult. William's father, John Barry, helped negotiate on behalf of his son. As Washington quickly learned, Barry was a tough negotiator. Washington needed additional negotiating advice and found that through the help of his friend George William Fairfax. Fairfax was blunt with Washington. Barry drove a hard bargain. But Washington should be patient and not settle with Barry on his terms. Washington listened and waited. Nevertheless, by 1771, Washington had started construction on the gristmill. Fairfax not only provided negotiation advice but also went further by helping him procure a millstone from the Fairfax quarry.

As construction on the gristmill commenced, Washington brought Harrison back into the fight when he took John and William Barry to court over the property. Harrison represented Washington in the suit, which was tried in Fairfax County Court in 1772. On August 20, 1772, the court ruled in George Washington's favor. He had won! With the gristmill built, operations could begin immediately without further issue.

Washington's Alexandria lawyer, Robert Harrison, helped him win the land that he needed to operate the gristmill without a lawsuit. His longtime friend and Alexandria trustee George William Fairfax helped him negotiate and complete the mill. Finally, Washington's flour and cornmeal could be sold to Alexandria merchants like George Gilpin and John Fitzgerald.[79] The construction of Washington's gristmill is a perfect example of how important Washington's Alexandria relationships were to him by the early 1770s. The town was nearly a quarter century old. Alexandria was established, and Washington's network was enmeshed in all aspects of his business, social, political, and religious life. He didn't realize on August 20, 1772, how much more he would need this extensive Alexandria network. The drumbeats of war were still faint in 1772. But they grew louder, and Washington would need Alexandria for the biggest challenge of his life: leading an army in a war for independence.

George Washington's reconstructed gristmill at Mount Vernon, originally built in 1771. The mill produced flour for commercial sale and exemplified Washington's innovative approach to agriculture. *Photo by the author.*

# Chapter 14

# WASHINGTON AND ALEXANDRIA MOBILIZE TOWARD WAR

George Washington's political talents were not defined by lofty rhetoric or long-form essays. In politics, George Washington could relate to his constituents. He shared their grievances. While he was principled, he was not an ideologue. He recognized that British taxes without colonial consent deprived him and his fellow Virginians of their constitutional rights. The Stamp Act (1765) crystallized the political understanding that taxation without representation was a form of despotism. The issue was resolved temporarily when the act was repealed in 1766. But the British parliament introduced other acts to raise funds from the colonists. Tension persisted for the next decade until the "shot heard 'round the world" at the Battles of Lexington and Concord on April 19, 1775.

Washington was politically influenced by his friend and fellow Alexandria trustee George Mason of Gunston Hall. Mason and Washington had a lot in common. Both were fourth-generation Virginians. Mason's father died when he was ten; George's father died when he was eleven. They both were farmers and had grown tobacco. They attended Pohick Church in Truro Parish and served on the vestry together. They both were members of the House of Burgesses from Fairfax County, although their time in office never overlapped. Mason was an investor in the Ohio Company along with Lawrence Washington and the Fairfaxes. Mason's interest in the Ohio Company made him a strong supporter of Washington's military service against the French during the French and Indian War. George

Portrait of George Mason, Virginia statesman, author of the Virginia Declaration of Rights and the Fairfax Resolves, and friend of George Washington. *Courtesy of Mount Vernon.*

Gunston Hall in Fairfax County, Virginia, home of George Mason, author of the Virginia Declaration of Rights and the Fairfax Resolves. *Photo by the author.*

Mason was close to the Fairfaxes of Belvoir. In fact, Gunston Hall was directly south of Belvoir, which made Mason a neighbor of the Fairfax family.

George Mason bought land in the Alexandria auction of 1749 and later became a town trustee. His interests in Alexandria were aligned with those of the Washington and Fairfax families. As a trustee and early lot owner, we can consider him one of the founders of the town alongside John Carlyle and William Ramsay. However, as we will cover in a later chapter, by 1788, Mason had a political falling out not only with George Washington but also with the city of Alexandria. Long before Mason's rift with Washington and Alexandria, he became a leader in helping to mobilize the town citizens toward war. First, he and Washington had frequent dialogue over political matters dating back to a non-importation agreement from 1769. This is one of the more noteworthy instances in which Mason and Washington took steps to oppose the British and pushback against policies that they deemed to be harmful. By 1769, George Washington had stopped planting tobacco at Mount Vernon and had switched to wheat, corn, and hemp. His relationship with Alexandria's merchants gave him latitude to protest Britain's mercantile system. The non-importation agreement was the equivalent of a colonial boycott. Washington and Mason worked to ensure that their fellow colonists were faithfully upholding the practice of non-importation.

The dramatic turning point in Virginia was not until 1774. The moment of political fervor can be traced back to the Boston Tea Party on December 16, 1773. The protest in Boston led to a response from the British government that was meant to single out the port of Boston and punish Massachusetts directly. The series of acts that followed in the spring of 1774 were called the Coercive or Intolerable Acts. While they were directed at Massachusetts, the acts galvanized the colonists. The American colonies were seized with a strong nationalism, which culminated in the first Continental Congress in Philadelphia that September.

In the intervening period between the closure of Boston Harbor and the first Continental Congress, there were important events in both Virginia and Alexandria. In fact, Alexandria can claim to have provided a strong catalyst for the first Continental Congress with the passage of a document called the Fairfax County Resolves.

The Fairfax County Resolves was one of many county resolves, which were drafted after the Virginia House of Burgesses dissolved in May 1774. As a burgess, Washington was in Williamsburg when the colonial assembly was shut down by Governor Dunmore due to colonial protests related to the Coercive Acts. Washington attended a day of fasting and prayer at Williamsburg's Bruton Parish on June 1, 1774. The House of Burgesses set a date to reconvene in August. In the meantime, each burgess was directed to return to his respective county and get a poll of the thoughts and opinions of his constituents.

Over the next two months, George Washington met with many of his constituents from Fairfax County and Alexandria. During most of July 1774, he spent his time in Alexandria. There was supposed to be a meeting early in the month that was postponed due to bad weather. But Washington still met and spoke with people at Arell's Tavern, which was in Alexandria's designated market square and adjacent to the Fairfax County Courthouse. On July 5, 1774, Washington wrote, "Went up to Alexandria to a Meeting of the Inhabitts. of this County. Dined at Arrells & lodgd at my own Ho[use]."[80]

Washington dined with leading men of the town, including Dr. William Brown. Brown was a highly educated Scotsman by background and studied at the University of Edinburgh. He was younger than Washington by sixteen years. Brown rented Washington's house on Cameron Street. But he was now living in a separate house because on July 6, Washington wrote, "Dined at Doctr. Brown's & returnd home in the Eveng."[81]

On the evening of July 17, 1774, George Mason stayed with Washington at Mount Vernon, and the two men finished drafting the document that would become the Fairfax County Resolves. Many of the specific resolutions were discussed in early July and approved by a committee in Alexandria. But

Plaque in Alexandria commemorating the Fairfax County Resolves, written by George Mason and George Washington, passed at the Fairfax County Courthouse on July 18, 1774. *Photo by the author.*

Mason put pen to paper and turned the Alexandria committee's ideas into a masterpiece of political thought. As night fell on the evening of July 17, Mason and Washington presumably discussed the final draft of the resolves. The following morning, July 18, Washington wrote, "Went up to Alexandria to a Meeting of the County."[82]

The meeting took place at the Fairfax County Courthouse. George Washington was chairman of the meeting in which the Fairfax County Resolves were read aloud and formally proposed. Washington's role as chairman was the first time in which he was "president" (i.e., presided over a political body). There is no other occasion prior to July 18, 1774, in which George Washington held a role as chairman of any political body (e.g., committee, assembly, convention, and so on). This fact cannot be understated because it was his experience in Alexandria that foreshadowed his future political role as president of the Constitutional Convention (1787) and president of the United States of America (1789–97).

The meeting brought together leading men of Alexandria, including John Carlyle, William Ramsay, George Gilpin, John Dalton, Robert Adam, Dr. William Rumney, and Dr. William Brown. Robert Harrison, Washington's talented lawyer, was secretary. The rector of Christ Church, Reverend Townsend Dade, was also present and signed the resolves. Twenty-four resolves were read aloud and proposed for signing. The resolves directly protested British actions not only against Boston and Massachusetts but also against all thirteen American colonies. The first resolve directly asserted that the colonists were not a "conquered people" and were descendants of the "conquerors." The language echoed the Stamp Act Resolutions from 1765. Mason revived the old debates and succinctly laid out that Americans were entitled to the same constitutional rights and privileges as any British subject. It didn't matter if they lived in Alexandria or London. With that being the case, it was resolved that taxation without representation was tyranny. The only legitimate government could be instituted among consenting citizens. These words echoed the words that Jefferson included in the Declaration of Independence almost two years later.

The Fairfax Resolves proposed a continental congress. They called for an end to the slave trade and outlined opposition in stark moral language that implied that each signer understood the slave system to be intrinsically wrong. They might not have been abolitionists, but the Fairfax Resolves articulated clear principles on which the system of slavery could be viewed as incompatible with the American founding. In total, there were twenty-five signers. George Washington knew them all and counted many of the signers as friends, especially the gentlemen from Alexandria.

Passage of the Fairfax Resolves was an important moment for George Washington and Alexandria. The Fairfax Resolves were adopted by the Virginia House of Burgesses two weeks later in Williamsburg. The call for a continental congress was accepted. Washington attended the First Continental Congress in Philadelphia, which met in September 1774. One year after the First Continental Congress met, America and Britain were at war.

At the beginning of the Revolutionary War and almost two years after he wrote the Fairfax Resolves, George Mason authored the Virginia Declaration of Rights, which was passed by the Virginia Convention in June 1776. The Virginia Declaration of Rights preceded the Declaration of Independence by one month. It was a foundational document influencing the Declaration of Independence's principal author, Thomas Jefferson. Furthermore, the Virginia Declaration of Rights provided a blueprint for the United States Bill of Rights (i.e., the first ten amendments of the U.S. Constitution), which were ratified in 1791.

While divisions at the Constitutional Convention eventually drove a wedge between Mason and Washington in 1787, their political beliefs and motivations were the same in 1774. By the summer of 1774, the political crisis in America moved the country closer to war. Washington and his Alexandria friends were not just being swept up in the times—they were leading the movement toward independence. Washington and Alexandria's next step was to organize the military effort to support the fight for independence.

# Chapter 15

# WASHINGTON AND ALEXANDRIA AT WAR

George Washington stopped in Alexandria on his way to the First Continental Congress in September 1774. While Washington and the other delegates in Philadelphia hoped to find a peaceful resolution, war seemed imminent. As tensions increased, Alexandria's leading citizens formed their own committees of correspondence and committees of safety. These committees became extensive networks and the equivalent of parallel governments that were designed to bring together different counties across Virginia to work together for the collective safety and benefit of Alexandria and its neighbors.

In terms of military strength, local militias were the foundation of America's defenses. The Fairfax County militia comprised many of the same men who signed the Fairfax Resolves, including prominent citizens like George Gilpin, William Rumney, Robert Harrison, and John Fitzgerald. In addition to the militia, the Fairfax County Independent Company was the first independent company formed in Virginia on September 21, 1774. There is a distinction between the two military units. The militia was tasked with local defenses. The Independent Companies were formed specifically in a "time of extreme danger, with the Indian Enemy in our County, and threat'ned with the Destruction of our Civil-rights, & Liberty."[83] The Virginia Independent Companies were used not only as defenses against the British but also during a period of hostilities with Indian tribes on the western frontier during what was known as "Dunmore's War," named after Virginia Governor Lord Dunmore. After the Second Continental Congress created the Continental army, the Fairfax County Independent Company and other independent companies from northern Virginia would be incorporated into the Third Virginia Regiment.

In the fall of 1774, the Fairfax Independent Company selected George Washington as its commanding officer. Washington accepted the command. On October 19, 1774, the Fairfax Independent Company wrote to Washington, who was then in Philadelphia for the First Continental Congress. In the letter, they requested "[a] pair of Colours, two Drums, two Fifes, and two Halberts, if they are to be had in Philadelphia; which may be sent round by the first Vessel for Alexandria."[84] Additionally, the Fairfax Independent Company uniforms were "turn'd up with Buff; with plain yellow metal Buttons, Buff Waist Coat & Breeches, & white Stockings."[85] Each member was to keep a "good Fire-lock & Bayonet, Sling Cartouch-Box, and Tomahawk."[86] Finally, each member was to "constantly keep by us a Stock of six pounds of Gunpowder, twenty pounds of Lead, and fifty Gun-flints, at the least."[87]

Along with the Fairfax Independent Company, other companies were formed in counties like Prince William. In fact, on November 13, 1774, Washington wrote, "Went up to Alexandria Church. In the Evening Colo. Blackburn Mr. Lee, & Mr. Richd. Graham came here as a Committee from the Prince Wm. Independ. Compy."[88] Perhaps this fact is what has given rise to the "tradition" that George Washington announced in the churchyard of Christ Church that "he believed the colonies should withdraw their allegiance from King George III."[89]

What is undeniable is that Washington and Alexandria were preparing for war before the Second Continental Congress began in May 1775. In 1775, George Washington went into Alexandria on six separate occasions to review the Fairfax Independent Company.[90] The first occasion was on January 16, 1775, when Washington "Went up to Alexandria to a review of the Independant Company & to choose a Com[mitt]ee for the County of Fairfax."[91] Washington referred specifically to committees that had been called for by the Continental Association to enforce a boycott of British imported goods. This was a use of economic pressure or an early form of sanctions being wielded against the British. It was taking place simultaneously with military preparations.

On April 15, 1775, George Washington wrote that he "Went up to Alexandria to the Muster of the Independt. Company."[92] Four days later, on April 19, 1775, the first shots of the American Revolution were fired at Lexington and Concord. While America had not formally declared

Portrait of George Washington by Charles Willson Peale, painted in 1772. *Courtesy of Mount Vernon.*

independence, war had begun. The following month, George Washington traveled to Philadelphia for the Second Continental Congress. He was a delegate representing Virginia. Like his previous trip to Philadelphia in 1774, he stopped in Alexandria. On May 4, 1775, Washington recorded in his diary, "Set out for the Congress at Phila. Dind in Alexa."[93] By May 1775, Alexandria had been preparing for almost a year since the British shut down the port of Boston. But in many ways, the seeds of war stretched back twenty years prior. Long before British troops were quartered in Boston homes, John Carlyle identified that the British "treated us as enemy country" and the "spawn of convicts."

Hostilities were not isolated to Massachusetts. Virginia's Governor Lord Dunmore had taken the gunpowder from the armory in Williamsburg. Militia units around Williamsburg took up arms against Dunmore's aggression. Against this backdrop of fighting in the northern and southern colonies, Washington arrived in Philadelphia in May 1775. Colonial delegates debated how to proceed in their collective defense. By mid-June, the delegates in Philadelphia had agreed to authorize a Continental army for the defense of Boston. The army's formal establishment was June 14, 1775, and is recognized as the official birthdate of the U.S. Army.

The following day, the Philadelphia delegates chose a commander-in-chief. George Washington had attended the proceedings in Boston "almost certainly" wearing the same "blue and buff uniform chosen for the Fairfax Independent Company."[94] Many historians have noted that George Washington's choice was a deliberate and not-so-subtle attempt to influence the delegates to choose him as commander-in-chief. However, the fact that George Washington was wearing a military uniform of "blue and buff" simply reflected the reality that Washington was already in command. He was commanding the Fairfax County Independent Company that had been formed by his friends in Alexandria. He had been active as commander, reviewing the company in Alexandria on six occasions within four months. Thus, there was no symbolism in the gesture. Washington was already on military duty as commanding officer of the Independent Company based in Alexandria.

Nevertheless, Washington's selection as commander-in-chief was only two days before another major battle occurred. This time, the battle was in the heart of Boston at Bunker Hill—or, more accurately, Breed's Hill. The British won a costly victory. They suffered significant casualties but did take the hill and held key terrain in Boston. However, they were under siege and surrounded by militia from Massachusetts. As a result, George Washington was sent to Boston to assume command, which he formally did on July 3, 1775.

## Washington Builds His Staff

Most military historians like to focus on specific battles and the fighting that occurred during the Revolutionary War. However, the battles themselves were quick albeit bloody affairs. Many battles of the Revolutionary War lasted an hour or less. In the interim period, much of what took place consisted of mundane matters, such as the administration and logistics of running an army. To raise an army from nothing was no easy feat. George Washington had significant experience and his own training during his five years of service in the French and Indian War. Furthermore, he had been working with the Fairfax Independent Company for more than eight months by the time he took command in Boston.

While the Siege of Boston began in June 1775, the next major engagement around Boston did not occur until March 1776. Over a nine-month period, George Washington built a new army outside of Boston. He dealt with the headaches of manpower and equipment just like he had in Alexandria during the French and Indian War. George Washington put together a staff that was known as his "military family." This consisted of several aides-de-camp and a military secretary, which was authorized by Congress. One of George Washington's first aides was Robert Harrison, who was Washington's lawyer from Alexandria and the son-in-law of the late George Johnston. Washington's selection of Harrison was consequential. Harrison had no formal military experience. He was commissioned as a lieutenant colonel. However, what he possessed was a sharp mind and an exceptional ability to communicate in writing. As much as Washington needed guns and manpower, he also needed people who could write communications that he delivered in the form of daily published orders. Also, he corresponded with subordinate officers and the Continental Congress extensively. As a result, the position that Harrison assumed was necessary to run an efficient and well-organized army. In selecting Harrison, Washington carried on a tradition of choosing one of his friends from Alexandria as an aide. If the reader will recall, Washington had relied on John Kirkpatrick from Alexandria as his aide and military secretary in the Virginia Regiment.

Robert Harrison was selected first as an aide but soon thereafter fulfilled the role of secretary, which he held until 1781. In 1781, personal circumstances pulled Harrison away from Washington's staff. However, he served under Washington throughout the most difficult periods of the Revolutionary War, beginning with the Siege of Boston through the New

York Campaign along with the Battles of Trenton and Princeton. In 1777, he was with Washington during the Battles of Brandywine and Germanton and then suffered through the winter at Valley Forge. He was with Washington during the Battle of Monmouth in the summer of 1778. He was also with Washington during the brutally cold winters in Morristown, New Jersey. Lieutenant Colonel Harrison does not always gain the same notoriety as aides like Alexander Hamilton or Joseph Reed. However, unlike Hamilton, Harrison never resigned out of frustration. Unlike Reed, Harrison never resigned because he wanted to pursue his political career. This is not to disparage the service of others but rather to illustrate how remarkable Harrison's own service was until he was personally no longer able to fulfill his duties in 1781.

Washington had such high regard for Harrison that he wanted to find other aides like him. As a result, there is a letter that George Washington wrote to Harrison asking whether his brother-in-law, George Johnston Jr., would be a good aide-de-camp. While Washington would have most likely known George Johnston Jr. through his father, it appears that Washington wanted to get a second opinion of him. Lieutenant Colonel Harrison confirmed that his brother-in-law was a good fit. Washington appointed George Johnston Jr. as an aide-de-camp in 1777 while the army camped at Morristown, New Jersey. Thus, during the Revolutionary War, Washington had two members of his military family from the same Alexandria family!

Sadly, George Johnston Jr. had a brief tenure. He died of yellow fever in the spring of 1777 only several months into his service as an aide-de-camp. His death must have been hard for both Washington and Harrison. George Johnston Jr. was not married and did not have any children when he died. Despite his brief tenure, the service of both George Johnston Jr. and Robert Harrison at the same time is one of the strongest examples of how significant Alexandrians were to Washington's service as commander-in-chief. While two of his aides from Alexandria were related by marriage, they were not the only two aides from Alexandria. In fact, during one of the low moments of the war, Washington sought an Alexandria friend whom he had known since 1769.

# Chapter 16

# THROUGH THE DARKEST DAYS OF THE WAR

The Siege of Boston culminated in March 1776. One of Washington's generals, a Boston bookseller named Henry Knox, arrived with cannons taken from Fort Ticonderoga. On March 4, 1776, Washington's Continentals took Dorchester Heights. In capturing this strategic terrain, Knox's cannons were positioned with a clear line of sight to fire on the British troops, "rendering [General] Howe's position untenable." The British evacuated Boston on March 17.[95]

Washington and his army had won a tactical victory. But General William Howe and the British were merely buying time and shifting their strategic approach. The conflict in America had escalated quickly, and the British marshaled their resources and manpower to smash a full-scale rebellion. The strategy shifted to New York. The goal was to take New York City and control the Hudson River. This would allow the British to cut off the New England colonies from the middle and southern colonies.

The New York Campaign was a formidable test for the American army and George Washington's leadership. In June 1776, Washington moved his army of fifteen thousand into "positions on Long Island and Manhattan in preparation for a major engagement with the larger British force."[96] There were multiple avenues of approach, creating a nightmare for defensive planning. Washington's forces were woefully outmanned. The British sent an "armada of 110 warships and transport boats" that carried heavily armed and well-trained Hessian soldiers and British regulars estimated to be nearly thirty thousand in number.[97] As the British fleet arrived and looked like "all London afloat," the Second Continental Congress passed a formal Declaration of Independence.[98] Two days after the "final text was approved on July 4," Washington had the declaration "read aloud to his army."[99] For General Washington, reading the Declaration of Independence must have stirred memories of the Fairfax Resolves being read at the courthouse in Alexandria. Washington would have undoubtedly recognized the tone and tenor of the document and heard the echoes of his friend George Mason.

On August 27, 1776, the British launched their attack with an amphibious assault on Long Island. They quickly broke through American defensive positions and gained key terrain. By nightfall, Washington's army was "hemmed in on Brooklyn Heights."[100] That evening, the American army narrowly escaped across the East River to Manhattan. Author David McCullough writes, "Orderly withdrawal of an army was considered one of the most difficult of all maneuvers."[101] He explains further, "Washington's ragtag amateur army was making a night withdrawal in perfect order and silence."[102] But this was not Washington's first experience leading the withdrawal of an army. His first experience dated to the withdrawal from Fort Necessity back to Alexandria in the summer of 1754. His second experience of a withdrawal under fire was during the disaster at the Monongahela as part of Braddock's Expedition in July 1755.

After taking Brooklyn Heights, the British then shifted their attention to Manhattan. On September 15, 1776, a "thunderous naval barrage" was unleashed on American defenses at Kip's Bay.[103] Following the barrage, the British deployed four thousand soldiers in eighty-four flatboats across the East River. They quickly gained a foothold on Manhattan Island. Unlike today, in 1776, Manhattan was still farmland and rural. The British cut off the southern part of the island that was more heavily populated, as it served as the main hub for New York's trade. Along with the many piers, wharves, and taverns, the population contained a significant number of Loyalists. In cutting off lower Manhattan, the British army then pursued Washington's army to the northern part of the island.

The jubilation from March 17, 1776, was now erased and shattered by what appeared to be an unstoppable military juggernaut. However, there was a glimmer of hope amid defeat. As the Continental army withdrew to Harlem Heights, George Washington was joined by the Third Virginia Regiment. This regiment was formed in Alexandria, Virginia, on December 28, 1775. Its recruits comprised many of the people who had been part of the Fairfax County Independent Company that Washington had trained in Alexandria. The Third Virginia's ranks included many prominent veterans, including America's fifth president, James Monroe, and future Supreme Court Justice John Marshall. Additionally, George Washington's second cousin, Captain William Washington, commanded the Sixth Company in the Third Virginia Regiment.

The Third Virginia saw initial action in Virginia throughout 1776. However, it was sent north to defend New York and join George Washington on Long Island. On September 16, 1776, the Virginians arrived in time to help launch a counterattack against the British at Harlem Heights. The outcome of the battle was enough to temporarily slow the British assault across Manhattan. However, one strategic consequence was that the victory improved morale after a string of defeats.

Washington's friends from Alexandria joined the fight at the right moment. As reinforcements, they were able to deliver Washington's army its first victory of the New York Campaign. One of Washington's friends was John Fitzgerald, who was a captain in the Third Virginia. Fitzgerald distinguished himself as a leader during the battle, so much so that he received a promotion. Due to the death of Major Leitch from the Third Virginia, Washington wrote a letter on October 5, 1776, to President of Congress John Hancock that informed him that Fitzgerald had been "appointed to the duty of Major."[104]

Fitzgerald was not a major for long and was soon pulled from the ranks of the Third Virginia. Washington saw greater use for his friend from Alexandria. Like Robert Harrison, his Alexandria friend and lawyer, he selected Fitzgerald to join his "military family" as an aide-de-camp. His selection took place in November 1776. Fitzgerald served on Washington's staff until 1778.

By December 1776, George Washington had two Alexandrians who were part of his military family. It was a pivotal moment in the fate of the army and America's war for independence. Despite the small victory at Harlem Heights, a series of defeats followed shortly thereafter. The first occurred at a battle in White Plains, New York, on October 28.[105] That defeat forced Washington's army into a retreat. But a more significant blow soon followed.

On November 16, the British surrounded and captured Fort Washington on Manhattan. The fall of Fort Washington was a devastating loss. The British captured nearly 2,800 American soldiers. They were hauled off to prison ships in New York Harbor. Many of them suffered sickness and starvation in inhumane conditions. But the British onslaught continued as they crossed the Hudson River and captured Fort Lee on November 20. General Washington led his army in a withdrawal deeper into New Jersey.

Finally, after reaching Trenton, New Jersey, on December 2, Washington and his army crossed the Delaware River for the first time into the safety of Pennsylvania. It was the first crossing of the Delaware River, but it would not be the last.

## Crossing the Delaware River

By Christmas 1776, Washington and his army needed a miracle. The New York Campaign had left the American army bruised and battered by the end of that year. The British and their Hessian conscripts were preparing for winter quarters. As Washington faced a potential exodus of troops from short-term enlistments, he looked for one final opportunity to give hope not only to his army but also to his fellow countrymen.

By December 25, 1776, the Third Virginia Regiment had formally fallen under Washington's direct command. One of the Patriots in the Third Virginia was a chaplain and surgeon named Reverend David Griffith. Reverend Griffith was originally from New York, but after his three years of service in the Continental army, he moved to Alexandria and became the rector of Christ Church Episcopal. If anyone was leading prayers on Christmas Day 1776, it would have been chaplains like Griffith. The army needed the help of the Almighty because Washington made one of the most important decisions of the entire war. He decided to personally lead his army across the Delaware River in a surprise attack against an isolated Hessian garrison located at Trenton, New Jersey.

As night fell, Washington's Alexandria aide-de-camp John Fitzgerald wrote, "It is fearfully cold and raw and a snow-storm setting in. The wind is northeast and beats in the faces of the men."[106] Fitzgerald noted that many of the men had no shoes. The army loaded into Durham boats to be transported across the Delaware River for the attack. Fitzgerald was with Washington and noted, "I have never seen Washington so determined as he is now….He stands on the bank of the stream, wrapped in his cloak, superintending the landing of his troops. He is calm and collected, but very determined."[107]

By the morning of December 26, the Continental army had made it across the river. They were behind schedule but getting closer to Trenton. One of the units that helped lead the attack was the Third Virginia. In fact, Washington's cousin Captain William Washington led fifty soldiers from the

Third Virginia in the attack. His second-in-command, Lieutenant James Monroe, was wounded when the battle began. Monroe was one of the few American casualties, and he spent ten days recovering at the home of the Coryell family, who owned a ferry on the Delaware River.

With the Third Virginia leading the assault and his Alexandria friends like Fitzgerald and Harrison by his side, Washington and his army closed in on the Hessian garrison and caught it by surprise. The Hessians awoke to fixed bayonets. They put up some small pockets of resistance, but the surprise attack overwhelmed them. They were quickly subdued by an American force that was cold and hungry yet determined.

After successfully winning the Battle of Trenton, Washington's army re-crossed the Delaware River back into Pennsylvania with a fresh supply of guns, ammunition, clothing, liquor, and approximately eight hundred Hessian prisoners.[108] However, after one brilliant victory, Washington decided to move his forces back into New Jersey. On January 2, 1777, the Americans won a battle at Assunpink Creek. The following day, January 3, 1777, a battle commenced outside the town of Princeton. Leading the battle was General Hugh Mercer, who had formerly been commanding officer of the Third Virginia before his promotion to brigadier general. Mercer died in the fighting at Princeton after being stabbed seven times with a bayonet.

As the fighting raged, Washington rallied his army against a British force led by Lieutenant Colonel Mawhood. As Washington rode on his white charger thirty yards from the British lines, his aide, Fitzgerald, was beside him. What happened next has become one of the more legendary stories about Washington in battle. After an exchange of volley fire, Fitzgerald "cover[ed] his face with his hat, certain that his commander, so conspicuous a target, was cut down."[109] But just as Washington had never been struck by a bullet during the Braddock Campaign in 1755, he was also unscathed during the attack at Princeton. As the white smoke dissipated, Washington turned to Fitzgerald and said, "Away my dear Colonel, and bring up the troops. The day is ours."[110] By the evening of January 3, 1777, Washington and his army had captured the town of Princeton and could claim a third victory within ten days.

The victories at Trenton, Assunpink Creek, and Princeton represented a dramatic turning point early in the war. When all hope appeared lost, Washington and his army snatched victory from the jaws of defeat. The army settled into winter quarters in Morristown, New Jersey, in 1777 with renewed hope that they would one day be independent. But that day was still far away, and many more battles and tough winters lay ahead.

# Chapter 17

# WASHINGTON CALLS DR. CRAIK

General Washington and his army shivered through a brutally cold winter in Morristown, New Jersey. As spring came and the weather warmed, America was still in the thick of its fight for independence. Despite the victories during the Ten Crucial Days, the challenges remained daunting. Among these were the abysmal state of medical care and a lack of well-trained doctors to fill the ranks. It was at this point that Washington turned to his good friend Dr. James Craik.

On April 26, 1777, Washington wrote to Craik to inform him that there were two medical jobs available in the army and that he could have either one that he chose. One job was senior physician and surgeon of the hospital. The other job was assistant director general. George Washington's offer was accompanied by a lengthy caveat. He didn't want Craik to feel pressured by his offer. Washington explained to Craik, "You know how far you may be benefitted, or injured, by such an appointment; and you must know, whether it is advisable, or practicable, for you to quit your Family, and practice, at this time. All these matters I am ignorant of; and request, as a friend, that my proposing this matter to you may have no influence upon your acceptance of it."[111]

Whatever pressure Craik might have felt, he did not indicate it in his return letter of reply. Craik's response brimmed with thanks and gratitude. He replied, "I shall think my self honoured by your procuring me the Deputy Director Genl Place in the middle department provided you think me Capable of discharging the Dutys of that Office."[112]

Home of Dr. James Craik on Duke Street in Alexandria. Craik was George Washington's close friend and personal physician. *Photo by the author.*

Craik did have to apologize because he was not able to accept the job immediately. The reason was that he had "some families under inoculation near Fredericksburg." Craik referred to the inoculation of patients against smallpox. Craik also provided Washington with an update on how Martha's granddaughter, Elizabeth Parke Custis, had recovered well from her smallpox inoculation. Additionally, Craik informed him that the enslaved laborers at Mount Vernon had all been inoculated against smallpox. Finally, Craik wrote, "Coll Mason has had it very favourably and is now well." Craik was also George Mason's personal physician, and this letter indicates that he may have helped inoculate Mason.

Craik's administration of smallpox inoculations was a result of an order from General Washington that mandated the entire Continental army be inoculated against smallpox. On February 6, 1777, Washington wrote a letter to Dr. William Shippen Jr. with the following directive: "Finding the Small pox to be spreading much and fearing that no precaution can prevent it from running through the whole of our Army, I have determined that the troops shall be inoculated."[113] From Craik's letter, we can see that the army policy led to other inoculations even among civilians. Furthermore, Washington's policy would have an impact on Alexandria, which played a prominent role as a location where soldiers were inoculated and recovered from the procedure. In fact, the Washington family doctor, William Rumney, eventually took over the position of supervising inoculations in Alexandria.

Craik accepted Washington's offer and decided to take the job of assistant director general. His timing was fortuitous. The warm weather was about to bring a new season of fighting. Craik would be present for the late summer and fall campaign as the British deployed their army to take Philadelphia. General Howe moved ten thousand soldiers by water from New York to the Chesapeake Bay, disembarking sixty miles south of Philadelphia at Head of Elk, Maryland. Howe's army clashed with the American army in southeast Pennsylvania at Brandywine Creek on September 11, 1777. The battle ultimately resulted in Washington and his army pulling back to Chester, Pennsylvania.

After the British won two smaller battles known as the Battle of the Clouds and Battle of Paoli, they finally marched triumphantly into Philadelphia on September 26, 1777. By this time, Congress had evacuated and fled west to York, Pennsylvania. Though struggling, George Washington and the Continental army launched a counterattack.[114] The battle took place on October 4, 1777, in Germantown, Pennsylvania. Washington sought an opportunity to attack a garrison of nearly nine thousand British soldiers. However, the attack was a mixture of complicated plans, poor command and control, and an ill-fated attempt to seize a British fortified position rather than bypass it. The Battle of Germantown had the potential to be another Trenton-style victory. However, the best that could be said was that it ended in a draw.

After an intense fall campaign, the American army settled into winter quarters twenty miles northwest of Philadelphia on a large plateau adjacent to a small forge that sat in a valley. The location was called "Valley Forge." The winter at Valley Forge tested the strength and spirit of the American army. George Washington worked every day to hold his army together. Between the fighting in late 1777 and the winter at Valley Forge, Washington now had Dr. James Craik, one of his best friends, by his side to help him and the American cause endure.

# Chapter 18

# DR. BROWN AT VALLEY FORGE

German American artist Emanuel Leutze painted an iconic image of George Washington standing defiantly on the bow of a Durham boat leading his army across the Delaware River. This image is how most people think about Washington's leadership during the Revolutionary War. While Washington undoubtedly led from the front in multiple battles, most of his daily leadership involved the minutiae of army management. Washington faced the same challenges that he encountered during the French and Indian War. Feeding, clothing, equipping, recruiting, and disciplining the army consumed Washington's attention as commander-in-chief.

Furthermore, keeping the army healthy was a daunting task. Medical care during the Revolutionary War does not always get as much study as the big battles and campaigns. However, illnesses like typhus, dysentery, and smallpox ravaged the army. In fact, it is estimated that disease killed at least double the number of soldiers killed in action.[115] As a result, Washington sought Dr. Craik's assistance and that of another prominent doctor from Alexandria, Dr. William Brown.

Brown, who was one of Washington's tenants at his house on Cameron Street and a signer of the Fairfax Resolves, had an impressive pedigree. He was educated in Scotland at the University of Edinburgh. He initially joined the Second Virginia Regiment and quickly distinguished himself. He took on new assignments as a surgeon of several mobile field hospitals known as "flying camps." He also briefly led a hospital in Bethlehem, Pennsylvania. This experience over two years of service eventually led to his promotion to

*Left*: Home of Dr. William Brown in Alexandria. Brown served as George Washington's physician during the Revolutionary War and was a trustee of the Alexandria Academy. *Photo by the author.*

*Opposite*: The Isaac Potts House at Valley Forge, used by George Washington as his headquarters during the winter encampment of 1777–78. *Photo by the author.*

director of hospitals in the Middle Department. It was as a hospital director that Washington relied on Brown most heavily. Brown's task was not easy. Hospitals were seen as a death sentence for the average soldier. Medical care lacked standardization, and sanitary practices were nonexistent. Few of the "doctors" had been to medical school, much less one as prestigious as the University of Edinburgh.

It is estimated that nearly 2,000 American soldiers died of disease during the winter at Valley Forge.[116] Meanwhile, it estimated that 1,425 soldiers deserted that winter.[117] A reported 1,967 soldiers were discharged from duty, and many of them were discharged due to illness.[118] The American army entered camp at Valley Forge with 12,000 soldiers and lost 5,415.[119] This rate of more than 40 percent indicates the scale of suffering that winter, especially from diseases.

As director of hospitals in the Middle Department, Brown oversaw a network of thirty hospitals in Pennsylvania from Lititz to Bethlehem. Brown tackled the poor conditions and lack of standardized medical care. His greatest attempt to find a solution to this problem was writing one of the first

medical pamphlets in the military. It was called the *American Pharmacopeia*, and it contained more than one hundred medical recommendations that included simple treatments and invasive surgeries.

By the spring of 1778, good news had reached the camp at Valley Forge. France signed a formal treaty with America on February 6, 1778, pledging to bring its vast military resources into the war for American independence. New recruits also came into camp. Meanwhile, these raw recruits and even veterans were being whipped into shape by a Prussian officer named Baron von Steuben. Von Steuben was promoted to major general and made inspector general of the army.

Between Dr. Brown's revamping of the medical system, France's entry into the war, new recruits, and a new training regimen, there was reason for optimism by the summer of 1778. The American army had been pushed to its limits but never broke. At a moment in which Washington's army needed a miracle to survive, the general had one of his Alexandria friends overseeing one of the most critical pieces of military infrastructure, the medical system. The situation was severe when Brown took over. It could have been worse. Brown was crucial in ensuring the survival of America's struggling army. The following year, Dr. Brown continued to serve by providing lectures for army surgeons. Finally, in 1780, Dr. Brown resigned. When he did, the Continental Congress issued the following statement: "Resolved, that Congress entertains a high opinion of the ability, integrity and past services of Dr. Wm. Brown, Physician-General, but as circumstances will no longer permit his continuance in the service, his resignation is accepted."[120]

After the Revolutionary War, Washington and Brown remained close friends. They dined together at each other's homes. They attended the same church. Furthermore, as we will see, Dr. Brown convinced Washington to help start one of the first free schools for poor and orphaned children in Alexandria. Brown and Washington were friends for nearly two decades until Brown's death in 1792.

# Chapter 19

# THE CONWAY CABAL

During the winter at Valley Forge, one of the most significant challenges to Washington's command came from within the ranks of the army. Shortly after the Battle of Germantown, General Horatio Gates led his army in upstate New York to a major victory over the British during the Saratoga Campaign. Gates's victory included capturing General John Burgoyne's five-thousand-man British army. This victory was particularly important given that the British had just captured Philadelphia.

What was great news in America's war for independence was simultaneously bad news for Washington professionally. On the heels of his two defeats and Gates's triumph, a confluence of congressmen along with Gates and several of his allies lost trust in Washington and took steps to place Gates in overall command of the Continental army.

Since it was an internal political fight rather than a major battle against the British, this affair is often overlooked. Nevertheless, it has become known historically as the "Conway Cabal." The name is derived from General Thomas Conway. Conway was Irish by birth but had served in the French army before the Revolutionary War. Conway was ambitious in his own right and wanted Gates to replace Washington.

A series of letters passed between Gates and Conway that indicated their mutual distrust and lack of faith in Washington's leadership. In one specific letter, Conway wrote to Gates, "Heaven has been determined to save your Country, or a weak General and bad Councellors would have ruined it."[121]

The existence of the letter was made known due to Gates's aide-de-camp, James Wilkinson, who had too much to drink and mentioned it to an officer on Lord Stirling's staff. Stirling brought this to the attention of Washington.

Gates and Conway were not alone in their attempt to undermine Washington's command. Several members of Congress were complicit as well. If it had been simply venting between two disgruntled officers, the affair might have had less significance. However, the Conway Cabal posed a challenge to Washington due to at least one or more high-profile congressmen working behind the scenes. Additionally, Thomas Mifflin, a former aide-de-camp to Washington, was also working against Washington. Mifflin was promoted to major general and quartermaster of the army, gaining significant influence in the covert power struggle.

The plot against Washington involved the establishment of a Board of War that was presided over by Gates, Conway, and Mifflin. Conway was appointed inspector general of the army. The Board of War was assigned the responsibility of overseeing Washington's activities at Valley Forge. With this power, the groundwork was set for Washington's removal by Congress and his replacement with Gates.

The Conway Cabal might have achieved its aims were it not for Washington's strong and entrenched network of allies, including his friends from Alexandria. More specifically, Dr. James Craik and Washington's aide-de-camp Lieutenant Colonel John Fitzgerald both helped unravel the plans against Washington.

Much as Dr. James Craik looked after George Washington's health, he was also watching his back and wrote a detailed letter that explained the depths of the plot against Washington. After traveling several days in Pennsylvania from Bethlehem to Lancaster, Craik wrote a letter to Washington on January 6, 1778. During that time, he discovered that Virginia Congressman Richard Henry Lee was involved in the conspiracy against Washington. This was significant because Washington had confided in Lee and often considered him an ally. Craik's confirmation of Lee's involvement was revelatory. Additionally, Dr. Craik confirmed that Thomas Mifflin, Washington's former aide-de-camp, was involved in the conspiracy.

In his letter to Washington, Dr. Craik explained, "My Attachment to your Person is Such, my Friendship is So Sincere that every Hint which has a tendency to hurt your Honour Wounds me most Sensibly." He followed up by telling Washington that he wanted him to be "apprized and have an eye towards" what Richard Henry Lee and Mifflin, especially, were up to. Furthermore, he was writing "from pure motives of Friendship."[122]

With Dr. Craik's intelligence, Washington and his supporters could plan their own effort to combat the cabal and keep General Washington in command. Much of the response was simply a matter of patience and not acting out of impulse. When Thomas Conway arrived at Valley Forge to assume his duties as inspector general, Washington and his general officers gave him an icy reception. They did not hinder his job, but the lack of cordiality vexed Conway and made him feel isolated in his position.

Dr. Craik's efforts were enhanced by those of John Fitzgerald, who took leave from Valley Forge in early February. Like Craik, he traveled extensively and personally met with President of Congress Henry Laurens of South Carolina. As the letter between Conway and Gates was known to Washington and his staff, Fitzgerald was able to discuss it with Laurens. Laurens informed Fitzgerald that he knew Daniel Roberdeau had a copy of the letter. Fitzgerald obtained an extract from the letter and sent it to George Washington on February 16, 1778. As a result, Fitzgerald corroborated the existence of the duplicitous letter between Gates and Conway.

Washington replied to Fitzgerald on February 28, 1778. He thanked him for the extracted piece of the letter and replied that he was hopeful "that matters have, & will, turn out very different to what that Party expected."[123] He knew that the plot was unraveling, and he could thank many people for supporting him through the incident, including Craik and Fitzgerald.

Washington concluded his letter to Fitzgerald by saying, "In a word, I have a good deal of reason to believe that the Machinations of this Junto will recoil upon their own heads, & be a means of bringing some matters to light which by getting me out of the way some of them thought to conceal—remember me in the most affectionate terms to all my old friends & acquaintance in Alexandria."[124]

Fitzgerald replied to Washington from Alexandria on March 17, 1778. In his letter, he mentioned meetings with other members of Congress, including Charles Carroll. Fitzgerald was able to tell Washington that the members of Congress whom he met with gave him the "strongest assurances" that no members of Congress had "utter[ed] a word which could be construed into the least disrespect for you," except for one. In fact, Fitzgerald reported that he thought Richard Henry Lee may have disrespected Washington in some closed conversations. If Lee had done that, Fitzgerald was told that he had gone silent under the overwhelming support Washington had received from "different quarters."[125]

Fitzgerald's exchange with Washington shows the extent to which his aide-de-camp had gone personally to advocate on his behalf. We know that

*Left*: Fitzgerald's warehouse on the Alexandria waterfront. Colonel John Fitzgerald, a merchant, was a close friend of George Washington's and served as his aide-de-camp during the Revolutionary War. *Photo by the author.*

*Below*: Plaque marking the home of Dr. James Craik. Craik served with Washington as a surgeon in the Continental army during the Revolutionary War and played a role in uncovering the Conway Cabal. *Photo by the author.*

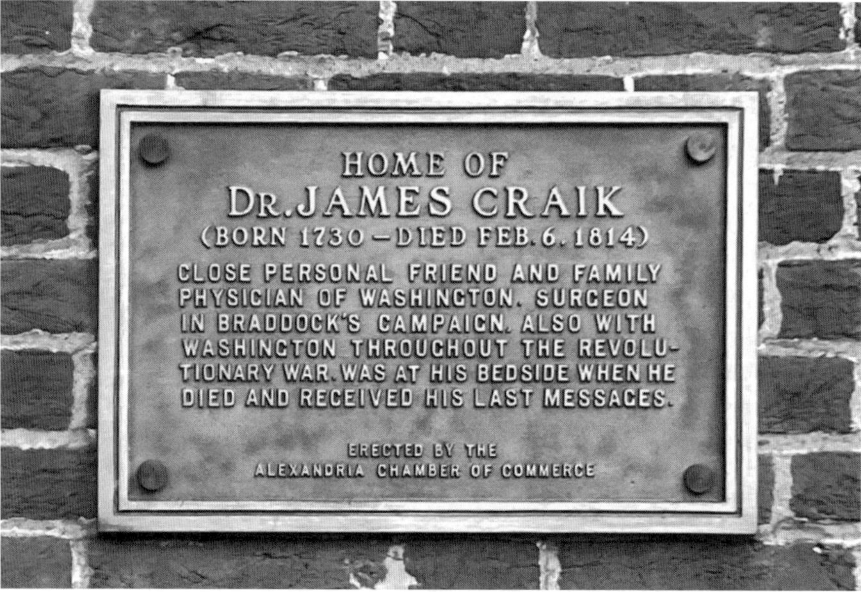


he met with multiple members of Congress and doubtless was able to speak in support of his commander-in-chief in his meetings with congressmen like Henry Laurens and Daniel Roberdeau. Furthermore, both Craik and Fitzgerald confirmed crucial evidence regarding the Conway Cabal.

The Conway Cabal speaks volumes about Washington's leadership. Despite his frustrations with the scheme against him, Washington displayed patience, self-control, and confidence in his ability to prevail. Washington did not act irrationally and chose to let his perpetrators unravel through their own blunders and missteps. Ultimately, they did. However, without the intelligence, lobbying, support, and encouragement of his close Alexandria friends, Washington might not have prevailed.

Besides Craik and Fitzgerald, it is also worth highlighting Daniel Roberdeau's support. Roberdeau was originally from Pennsylvania and represented Pennsylvania in Congress at that time. However, he later moved to Alexandria after the Revolutionary War. He lived in a stately Federal-style home on South Lee Street (then Water Street). Roberdeau was a supporter of Washington and worked with him to set up a network of militiamen known as the "flying camp." Considering Roberdeau's post–Revolutionary War move to Alexandria, he can be counted as one of the many Alexandrians who supported Washington both during the Revolutionary War and specifically to overcome the Conway Cabal.

As the plot against Washington dissolved, he could remain focused on the survival of his army. Fitzgerald's letter to Washington concluded by saying, "Your friends [in Alexandria] receive your Complimts with the highest Sense of Gratitude."[126] When Washington read Fitzgerald's letter in March 1778, the issue of survival was still in doubt. However, there was one issue that his Alexandria friends helped put to rest. Washington remained commander-in-chief and would do so until the war's conclusion in 1783.

# Chapter 20

## HENRY "LIGHT-HORSE HARRY" LEE

The Lees of Virginia were a sprawling dynasty descended from one of the prominent first Virginia families. Richard Henry Lee and Francis Lightfoot Lee were both powerful members of the Lee family and the only two brothers who signed the Declaration of Independence.

As evidenced by the Conway Cabal, George Washington and Richard Henry Lee had a rocky political relationship. That relationship would not heal with time, and further disagreements arose over the U.S. Constitution. Nevertheless, there was another branch of the large Lee family that was intensely loyal to George Washington. The Lees who descended from Henry Lee II included Henry Lee III, Charles Lee, Richard Bland Lee I, and Edmund Jennings Lee. Each one of these Lees lived in Alexandria, Virginia, at some point in time.

Their father, Henry Lee II, was a cousin of Richard Henry Lee and Francis Lightfoot Lee. This meant that the four sons were second cousins of the two signers of the Declaration of Independence. However, they were all politically aligned with George Washington and became staunch Federalists. Charles Lee and Richard Bland Lee were vital political allies to Washington during Washington's presidency.

Furthermore, during the winter encampment at Valley Forge, Henry Lee III played a crucial role in the survival of Washington's army. Henry Lee was a smart and aggressive officer from Leesylvania in Prince William County, Virginia. He attended the College of New Jersey (Princeton University) and received instruction under the teaching of the college's president, Reverend

Portrait of Henry "Light-Horse Harry" Lee (1756–1818), Revolutionary War cavalry officer, governor of Virginia, and father of Robert E. Lee. A close friend of George Washington's, Lee delivered Washington's famous eulogy in 1799. *Courtesy of Encyclopedia Virginia.*

John Witherspoon, who was a signer of the Declaration of Independence. Lee's attendance at Princeton overlapped with America's fourth president, James Madison.

After the war broke out in 1775, Henry Lee quickly signed up to fight for independence. Like many young Virginia gentlemen, Lee was raised on horseback and was a gifted rider. As a result, he was recruited into a company known as the First Continental Light Dragoons. He became a captain in the Light Dragoons. The Dragoons were created for the purpose of serving as cavalry. The primary responsibility of cavalry was to provide military intelligence. They screened friendly troop movements while simultaneously reporting enemy troop movements. The Light Dragoons were authorized by Congress after the losses in the New York Campaign in 1776. Washington recognized that many of the failures of his army were due to poor intelligence. Light Dragoons that acted as cavalry could help solve this problem.

As a captain in the Light Dragoons, Lee served under Washington during the Battles of Brandywine and Germantown. He was with the army during the winter at Valley Forge. Captain Lee remained active throughout the winter. He conducted bold raids on British supply lines to provide essential food and provisions to the starving soldiers at Valley Forge.

During one such raid, Lee and several of his soldiers were trapped in a house and surrounded by a much larger force of British cavalry. It could have been the end of Lee had it not been for a quick deception plan. Lee had his soldiers fire at the British in a rotating volley while simultaneously shouting and moving throughout the house. The goal was to make the British think that there was a much larger force inside the house. The ruse succeeded. The British cavalry pulled back. Lee and his half-dozen soldiers evaded capture and lived to fight another day.

Washington publicly praised Lee in an order dated January 20, 1778. The order stated, "The Commander in Chief returns his warmest thanks to Captn Lee & Officers & men of his Troop for the Victory which by their superior Bravery and Address they gain'd over a party of the Enemys dragoons."[127] On the same day, Washington followed up with a personal note to Lee: "My dear Lee, Altho I have given you my thanks in the general Orders of this day for the late instance of your gallant behaviour I cannot resist the Inclination I feel to repeat them again in this manner."[128]

Lee was promoted to major that same year. During that winter, Washington's army was being trained by a Prussian officer named Baron Friedrich Wilhelm von Steuben. Under Von Steuben's training, the army became more disciplined and learned sound tactical doctrine. At the same time, Lee was learning from experience and developing innovative cavalry tactics. The American army was not even three years old by the winter of 1778, which meant American officers, like Lee, learned military doctrine not in a book but through experience.

From his raids, Lee experimented with cavalry executing more than simple reconnaissance missions. He used cavalry like infantry, setting the foundation for a unit that combined both the speed of cavalry and heavy firepower from the infantry. The combined infantry and cavalry unit was called Lee's Legion. While these tactics had been tried in the European theater, Lee developed them in America. One of the first tests of his new tactic was during the Battle of Paulus Hook in September 1779. The battle was an American victory and a triumph for Lee. However, there was an internal issue that involved a dispute over rank. Lee had his detractors and was accused of misconduct during the Paulus Hook raid. While he was initially court-martialed for his actions, he had the support of George Washington. As a result, Lee was acquitted of all charges. In fact, the Continental Congress presented him with a gold medal for his actions at Paulus Hook.

Plaque on Cameron Street marking the home of Henry "Light-Horse Harry" Lee, Revolutionary War cavalry officer and later governor of Virginia. Lee moved into the house in 1810 after spending a year in debtors' prison. *Photo by the author.*

After the British captured Charleston* on May 12, 1780, Lee was deployed to South Carolina. He served under General Nathanael Greene through 1781. The fighting in the Carolinas was well suited for Lee's Legion. Lee distinguished himself as a leader and served alongside Francis Marion (the "Swamp Fox"). Lee and Marion partnered on daring raids throughout South Carolina. Furthermore, Lee commanded his Legion during several of the most important battles, including Guilford Courthouse and Eutaw Springs, as well as sieges such as Ninety-Six and Yorktown.

After the Revolutionary War, Henry Lee bought extensive property in Alexandria, Virginia. Henry Lee and his brothers became an integral part of the political and social fabric of Alexandria and also trusted friends to George Washington. Henry Lee and Washington were friends until the day Washington died in December 1799. The underpinnings of their friendship stretched back two decades to a low moment in the American Revolution when Lee helped Washington's cold and struggling army stay alive at Valley Forge.

* It was spelled "Charlestown" at this point in history, but for ease of reading, the modern spelling will be used throughout.

# Chapter 21

# THE BATTLE OF MONMOUTH

By the spring of 1778, events had shifted in America's favor. News arrived in the camp at Valley Forge that commissioners in France led by Benjamin Franklin had brokered a formal treaty with France to bring its military might and money into the war as an ally of America. Cheers erupted throughout the camp when the news arrived. It had been a difficult winter, but the army had endured. While slightly more than 40 percent of the army had died, deserted, or been discharged, new recruits had come in. Under Major General Friedrich von Steuben, the new recruits and veterans underwent extensive drills that trained them into a fine fighting force.

Washington yearned for an opportunity to attack. He didn't have to wait long. The British decided to leave Philadelphia and return their forces to New York. More importantly, they opted to march overland rather than return to the Head of Elk and be transported on the sea. As a result, the British moved their ten-thousand-man army and supply trains through New Jersey in June 1778.

Washington devised a plan to strike at the British army before it could make it safely back to New York City. On June 28, 1778, the battle took place in New Jersey near Monmouth Courthouse on a sweltering, humid day. As American soldiers marched toward Monmouth, many collapsed and died of heat exhaustion before the fighting began.

As Washington drew up his plan of attack, he tasked General Charles Lee (no relation to Henry Lee) with launching the first part of the attack. However, early in the battle, Washington noticed that soldiers, who were supposed to be attacking, were instead retreating. Washington was accompanied by his Alexandria aides John Fitzgerald and Robert Harrison. In his book *George Washington's Indispensable Men*, author Arthur S. Lefkowitz writes, "Harrison and Fitzgerald offered to go ahead and find out what was happening."[129] Harrison and Fitzgerald rode off to find General Lee's position. As they did, both of Washington's Alexandria aides witnessed more troops fleeing from the battlefield. Finally, Lefkowitz writes, "As Harrison and Fitzgerald rode closer to the village they came across General Lee sitting on horseback near a fence and watching the British advance."[130]

Harrison and Fitzgerald briefly spoke with Lee's aides to get an answer. They then rode forward to scout the enemy position. When they did, they were nearly overwhelmed by a force of British light infantry and grenadiers. Both aides hastily retreated and went back to warn Washington that the enemy was close.

While Harrison and Fitzgerald looked for their commander, Washington came across Charles Lee. Enraged by Lee's failure to attack, Washington demanded an explanation. But Lee was not able to give a proper justification. Washington shouted at his second-in-command, shocking all who witnessed his furious invective against Lee. Washington fired him on the spot. Moments after Lee was relieved, Fitzgerald "found Washington and reported what Harrison and he had seen." The enemy was attacking.

Fitzgerald's report was enough to bring Washington back to his senses. If Lee wouldn't lead the attack, Washington would do it himself. Washington found two regiments retreating and immediately directed them back into the fight. The battle was not entirely lost. While the element of surprise was gone, Washington's army was able to form ranks and fought hard against the British. The two sides battled to a tactical draw. However, there was a strategic victory that Washington himself may not have fully comprehended. Washington's army performed admirably. They looked, acted, and fought like professionals. While moral victories might not mean much in sports, they are important in war. Moral victories influence the hearts and minds of the country's citizens and lift the confidence of its army.

Washington wanted a tactically brilliant victory, but what he got was enough to build momentum into the next phase of the war. That phase gave Washington reason for optimism. The French had joined the American cause. The British were going to have to reassess their strategy. Ultimately, they would look to the southern colonies as their next target.

In the fallout from the Battle of Monmouth, Washington's firing of Lee was significant. Whether Lee directly obfuscated Washington's plans is a matter of historic debate. Defenders of Lee's actions believe that he was executing Washington's plan but doing so in a way that he thought most practical. Regardless of which side one chooses to take, the historic record is clear that George Washington believed "Lee's conduct as either cowardly or an insubordinate effort."[131] Relieving Lee of his command in the middle of the battle was the culmination of Washington's frustrations with Lee.

Fitzgerald's involvement in the spat showed how essential Washington's aides were to him. It is one of the clearest examples of how Washington used his aides as his eyes and ears on the battlefield. Their ability to quickly move and communicate both with subordinate officers was key. This allowed Washington to make timely decisions. In this case, the intelligence that Fitzgerald brought directly to Washington allowed him to stop a retreat that might have cost him the battle.

Unfortunately, Fitzgerald was injured at the Battle of Monmouth. He had served as Washington's aide-de-camp since November 1776. His contributions were of immense importance during the triumphs at Trenton and Princeton and the challenges faced at Valley Forge and the Conway Cabal. After leaving the army in 1778, Fitzgerald returned to Alexandria. He went back into business as a merchant but was also involved in helping protect the town from a British attack up the Potomac River. Fitzgerald and Washington reunited after the war, and their lives remained closely intertwined professionally and personally.

However, there was one final contribution that Fitzgerald made to help Washington during the Revolutionary War. General Lee requested a court-martial to clear his name of wrongdoing. Fitzgerald was called to testify at his court-martial. Robert Harrison also testified. According to Lefkowitz, "All of Washington's aides, Harrison, Hamilton, Fitzgerald, Laurens, Meade, McHenry, and Tilghman, gave damaging testimony against Lee."[132] General Lee never returned to command in the Continental army. The incident at Monmouth Courthouse and the court-marital of Lee removed another internal headache for General Washington. It was one less obstruction on the way to securing America's independence.[133]

# Chapter 22

# ALEXANDRIA AND THE ROAD TO YORKTOWN

During the Revolutionary War, Alexandria reprised its role as a center of recruiting, logistics, and medical care, as it had done during the French and Indian War. Just as George Washington recovered from his illness at the home of John Carlyle in 1757, many soldiers were sent to Alexandria to be treated for sickness and disease prevention. Early in the war, Alexandria's inoculations were overseen by Dr. Rickman. However, Rickman was relieved of command in 1778. Taking his place was Dr. William Rumney, Washington's physician and friend from before the Revolutionary War. Rumney's service in the war continued in Alexandria as a doctor.[134]

Furthermore, Dr. Rumney also commanded the Fairfax County militia. As the British moved on Philadelphia, Colonel Rumney mobilized his company to come to Washington's defense. They made it to York, Pennsylvania, but ultimately returned to Alexandria. In returning to Alexandria, they had an important job in the defenses of the Potomac River. While Washington, D.C., did not yet exist, Alexandria was a vital port city. By 1779, the British had revamped their strategy and shifted their focus of the war's effort to the southern colonies. As a result, the threat posed to Alexandria increased.

In December 1779, the British sent a flotilla from New York City to Charleston, South Carolina. The Siege of Charleston began on February 11, 1780. By May 12, 1780, the British had captured Charleston and imprisoned a force of five thousand Americans. The fall of Charleston was a blow to America's fight for independence. It kicked off a new phase of the war that lasted nearly two years until the American victory at Yorktown.[135]

In the interim period, Virginia was also targeted as part of the southern strategy. In 1780, Governor Thomas Jefferson moved the capital from Williamsburg to Richmond. During this time, Alexandria's role as a center of logistics accelerated. George Washington authorized Alexandria to become one of four critical supply depots in Virginia. Each depot had to maintain a quota of supplies, and Alexandria's quota included "40,000 gallons of rum, 80 tons of hay, and 40,000 bushels of corn."[136]

Another significant change also occurred in 1779 when the Virginia General Assembly formally incorporated Alexandria as a city with a new form of government, including a city council and elected mayor. This replaced the former system of town trustees. The transition to the new government occurred in 1780 as Alexandria took on its role as supply depot. This led to big changes for the city and the merchant class that worked to fulfill the quota of supplies. The first elected mayor was Colonel Robert T. Hooe, formerly of Maryland and a militia officer. Hooe had a wharf built at the foot of Duke Street. He was a well-known merchant with a firm called Jenifer & Hooe and later with a firm called Hooe & Harrison. Hooe used his vast resources, notably his ships, to procure the essential supplies of liquor and gunpowder.

Furthermore, there were other members of the Alexandria merchant class who worked within the city to fulfill Alexandria's depot quota. John Fitzgerald, Washington's former aide-de-camp, was back in Alexandria and had returned to his merchant business. When the British threatened Virginia in 1780, Virginia Governor Thomas Jefferson sent Fitzgerald a letter with an urgent request for guns and ammo. The letter read, "Being much distressed for Cartridge boxes, and cartridge paper for muskets (most particularly the latter article) we find it necessary to purchase up immediately as much of both as we can. Having no particular agent in the neighborhood of Alexandria, we take the liberty of asking your exertions on behalf of the public on this occasion."[137]

Fitzgerald was also joined by a fellow Continental Line officer named James Hendricks. Hendricks, like Fitzgerald, returned to Alexandria after being wounded in a battle, specifically the Battle of Germantown. Like Fitzgerald and Hooe, Hendricks helped supply the Continental army as the war shifted to the southern theater. Hendricks was the second elected mayor of Alexandria after Hooe. These merchants and others had their work cut out for them as the fighting intensified in the Carolinas.

After the British capture of Charleston, they won subsequent victories, including at Waxhaws and Camden. During the latter battle, General

Horatio Gates fled the battlefield and was relieved of command. Washington replaced Gates with General Nathanael Greene. As Greene traveled south to the Carolinas, he was accompanied by General Friedrich von Steuben. Greene and Von Steuben made a critical stop in Alexandria on their way south. Since Alexandria was a vital city in the military supply chain, Greene and Von Steuben relied on the city to help feed, clothe, and arm the Continental army. After the stop in Alexandria, Greene continued to South Carolina. Von Steuben remained in Virginia in Chesterfield County, where he established a headquarters and another supply depot.

In December 1780, the British sent Benedict Arnold, the American hero turned traitor, to Virginia to capture Richmond. Arnold was now a brigadier general in the British army and led a menacing force that stormed from Hampton Roads to Richmond. Jefferson, who had already relocated the capital to Richmond, fled west to avoid capture. In response, General Washington sent the Marquis de Lafayette to Virginia with a force of 1,200 men to fight and, hopefully, capture Arnold.

In early April 1781, when Washington ordered Lafayette to Virginia, British ships made a move toward Alexandria with the intention of burning the town. According to a letter from Peter Wagener to Thomas Jefferson, British vessels were "cruising up and down the [Potomac]" and Alexandria was in a "defenseless situation." Nevertheless, Alexandrians rallied to the defenses of the embattled port city. This included Fitzgerald and Hendricks. Wagener also recounted sending a company of artillery under Captain Conway, Taylor, Harper, and Robertson.[138] While the Alexandrians were outnumbered, they made a show of force that "frightened" the enemy and convinced them to abandon their plans for Alexandria.[139] George Mason also wrote about this incident as follows: "On the 12th, Alexandria was in much confusion at the approach of the enemy's fleet….Colonel Fitzgerald, however, made such a bold show that the British did not land."[140]

Thanks to the courage of Alexandrians, they were able to ward off an attack on their vital port city. Local militia then arrived, and Jefferson approved cannon reinforcements to defend the city. A letter from Robert Mitchell to Thomas Jefferson from April 12, 1781, indicated that the city was being reinforced with militia as 1,200 Pennsylvania Line troops were expected the next day. On April 21, Lafayette reached Alexandria to take command of the 1,200 Pennsylvanians.

Like Greene and Von Steuben, Lafayette stopped in Alexandria to acquire necessary supplies and equip his newly formed unit to battle the British. It was going to be a tough fight against a British opponent that had gained the upper hand. However, as Lafayette deployed from Alexandria in May, he and his army were prepared to counterattack the British and secure Virginia. Lafayette was an exceptional leader, and he was able to drive the British from central Virginia and ultimately force them back to the York peninsula.

By the fall of 1781, the British had established a defensive position in Yorktown, Virginia. Lafayette immediately recognized the vulnerability of this position. Furthermore, events moved rapidly toward the climax of the Virginia Campaign. A French fleet under Admiral de Grasse was on its way to Hampton Roads from Santo Domingo. It was scheduled to arrive by early September 1781. As a result, Washington and his army abandoned plans to try to capture New York City. They were on their way to Virginia, specifically Yorktown.

# Chapter 23

# YORKTOWN AND AMERICAN VICTORY

George Washington had envisioned a grand attack against the British in New York City. In his mind, he saw New York as the key to victory. However, by 1781, the bulk of the fighting raged in the South between the Carolinas and Virginia. After the British took Charleston in 1780, their southern strategy appeared to be a wise decision. The British had the upper hand by late 1780. However, with the appointment of General Greene as commander of the army in the South, the Americans were able to regain their strength under Greene's effective leadership. American victories at Kings Mountain on October 7, 1780, and Cowpens on January 17, 1781, helped turn the tide. These victories were followed by a bloody engagement that took place on March 15, 1781, at Guilford Courthouse near present-day Greensboro, North Carolina.

The Battle of Guilford Courthouse was not a triumphant American victory. In fact, it was considered a tactical victory for the British under General Cornwallis. However, the British won the battle at a high cost. After the Battle of Guilford Courthouse, Cornwallis made the decision to recover his army in Wilmington, North Carolina. He then moved to Virginia to link up with British forces under Benedict Arnold. As General Greene was able to win significant battles in the Carolinas and rebuild his strength, Cornwallis concluded that Virginia, with its major supply centers such as Alexandria, provided the critical lifeline for Greene's army. Thus, Virginia was his target. That decision drove him toward a peninsula situated between the rivers James and York.

Portrait of the Marquis de Lafayette by Charles Willson Peale, 1779. *Washington-Custis-Lee Collection, Washington and Lee University, Lexington, Virginia.*

Meanwhile, George Washington had been making plans with French forces under the Comte de Rochambeau. In anticipation of the French arrival in Rhode Island, Washington dispatched Dr. Craik to Rhode Island to find suitable medical facilities, including a hospital for the French forces. While many historians focus on whether George Washington won or lost a particular battle to assess his skills as a general, Washington's use of Craik and his doctors from Alexandria shows that he was concerned with important administrative and logistics needs such as medical care. Considering the extent to which sickness and disease impaired the army, this action and Craik's work deserve more recognition.

When Washington received word of the French fleet coming to Hampton Roads by September 1781, he scrapped his plans to retake New York City. Lafayette also urged Washington to move the army to Virginia. By August 1781, George Washington and the French army had moved overland from New York to Virginia. Again, Alexandria provided a stop along the journey and a chance for the army to rest and resupply. Many of the leading merchants of Alexandria were contracted to provide supplies for Washington's army. On September 15, 1781, Washington was stationed outside Yorktown and wrote a letter to Alexandria merchant James Hendricks. In the letter, Washington explained a lack of bread for the army: "I have therefore to request in the most earnest Terms that you will use every Effort in your Power to send down all the Flour within your Reach."[141] Hendricks replied in a letter dated September 20, 1781, and told Washington that he had procured a craft "capable of carrying four Hundred Barrels of flour."[142] Furthermore, he also explained he was getting a brig from Baltimore that could carry 170 barrels, and he was working with a "French agent" to deliver another 200 barrels of flour. Finally, Hendricks was also trying to purchase an additional 500 barrels of flour.[143] It was a well-timed letter because Alexandria was about to welcome a large French force.

Rochambeau's troops camped in Alexandria September 24–26, 1781. Rochambeau's encampment in Alexandria shows that Alexandria was integrated into one of four separate approach marches made by the combined American and French army on the way to Yorktown. By late

September 1781, the bulk of the army arrived in Williamsburg and was within striking distance of the British defenses at Yorktown. In Williamsburg, Dr. Craik worked to set up an extensive network of hospitals just as he had done in Rhode Island. This was not an easy task, as the job entailed finding suitable homes and public spaces. It involved negotiating with local people and elected officials. Asking people to give up their private residence for sick soldiers was not an easy sell, but Craik worked tirelessly to ensure that the army was properly supported to begin the Siege of Yorktown.

The siege kicked off in early October. Washington's army used conventional siege tactics that involved building a system of trenches that could position artillery cannons closer to the British defensive positions. Siege warfare was a tough and arduous task. However, if done properly, the attacking unit often had an advantage. For the besieged, the only hope was to be resupplied and reinforced. If the unit was isolated and cut off from any supplies or additional troops, then it was typically a matter of time before they would raise the white flag and ask for terms of surrender.

For Cornwallis and the British, American artillery pounded on their defensive positions as they received the news that there would be no reinforcements. The French navy had won a thrilling victory at the Battle of the Capes in early September. The British could not expect a resupply or any assistance from their own navy. They were isolated and cut off. American and French forces inched closer each day as they dug trenches in a zigzag pattern and established artillery positions that could pulverize the British redoubts. The noose quickly tightened around the neck of the British army.

Finally, on the dark night of October 14, 1781, American and French forces attacked British positions with fixed bayonets. Lafayette led troops in an attack on redoubt number nine. Hamilton had his moment of glory as he led an assault that captured redoubt number ten. Americans stormed over the defensive positions with a ferocious determination to win the battle and force the British to capitulate. On October 17, 1781, they did just that. A British officer waved a white flag. Cornwallis was ready to discuss terms of surrender.

Negotiations took place at the Moore House. The terms of surrender were the same as what the British had offered the American army in Charleston, South Carolina. On October 19, 1781, the British formally surrendered. For Cornwallis, it was a humiliating blow. He feigned illness on the day of surrender. His second in command presented his sword to Rochambeau during the surrender. Rochambeau gestured to Washington. Washington gestured to his second in command, General Lincoln.

*Left*: Historical marker in Alexandria noting the Washington-Rochambeau Route, marking the French and American encampment on the road to the Siege of Yorktown in 1781. *Photo by the author.*

*Opposite*: The Moore House in Yorktown, Virginia, where negotiations for the British surrender took place in 1781, effectively ending major combat in the Revolutionary War. *Photo by the author.*

War had raged for six years. By the end of 1781, victory was inevitable. Yorktown sealed the British fate and ensured American independence. It would take two more years for treaty negotiations to be discussed and signed. In the aftermath of Yorktown, Washington received congratulations from leading citizens of Alexandria. However, their congratulations also included a note of condolence. Unfortunately, Washington's stepson, Jacky Custis, died due to camp fever shortly after the Yorktown victory.[144] Jacky's death illustrates the terrible cost of war that resulted from sickness and disease. It underscores the importance of medical care and speaks to why Washington valued the service of Alexandria doctors like James Craik, William Rumney, and William Brown. He understood that the work his friends did to alleviate the suffering of his army was as important as triumphs on the battlefield.

Despite his personal losses, Washington kept the army together for the next two years. In fact, several of the challenges during that time included a potential mutiny within the army. While encamped in Newburgh, New York, in March 1783, Washington personally thwarted an insurrection

that had been planned among disgruntled officers. On March 15, 1783, Washington made an appeal to his officers to remember the work that they had accomplished and the sacrifices that they had made over the last eight years. He made a dramatic gesture by putting on his eyeglasses to read a letter of support from Joseph Jones, a Virginia congressman.[145] No one had seen Washington wear glasses. As he put them on, Washington humbly said, "Gentlemen, you will permit me to put on my spectacles, for, I have grown not only gray, but almost blind in the service of my country."[146] This personal touch brought tears to the eyes of the officers assembled. Washington reminded them how much he had personally sacrificed. His leadership broke the back of a potential insurrection.

The army held together until the British left New York on November 25, 1783, "Evacuation Day." On December 4, 1783, Washington gave a fond farewell to his officers at a tavern in New York called Fraunces Tavern. After his farewell, he was on his way to Annapolis, Maryland, to meet with Congress and formally resign his commission.

# Chapter 24

## RETURNING HOME

On December 23, 1783, George Washington entered the Maryland Statehouse in Annapolis. America had won the war, and Washington offered his resignation by stating, "Having finished the work assigned me. I retire from the great theatre of Action….I here offer my Commission, and take my leave of all the enjoyments of public life."[147] Congress purposely did not applaud. Washington's resignation was a matter of duty. However, as Washington left, the members stood and removed their hats in a gesture of respect. George Washington recognized that he served at the pleasure of Congress and by extension at the pleasure of the people. It was a remarkable moment in American history as well as world history. Washington did what most revolutionary leaders never did: he handed power back.

As he retired from public life, he set his attention on returning to the pleasures of private life. He was ready to enjoy his life at Mount Vernon. As he went home to Mount Vernon, Washington was also going back to his hometown of Alexandria. He was able to have dinner at the homes of his friends. He attended services at Christ Church and enjoyed the many taverns in Alexandria on social occasions.

Only eight days after Washington resigned his commission, he stepped into Duvall's Tavern in Alexandria on December 31, 1783. Alexandria feted George Washington, which means the city honored him and his service. Friends and fellow veterans joined him. Alexandria's mayor, Richard Conway, led thirteen toasts to celebrate. Conway was a wealthy Alexandria merchant who was active in Alexandria politics and business.

He was also a veteran of the Revolutionary War, as he served as a captain in the Continental army. As a result, Mayor Conway epitomized so many of Washington's friends in Alexandria. Six years later, Conway would play a significant role in Washington's return to service and his trip to New York City for his inauguration on April 30, 1789.

On New Year's Eve 1783, the celebration at Duvall's Tavern in Alexandria held equal significance to Washington's farewell to his officers at Fraunces Tavern in New York City. Fraunces Tavern was the site of one of the last formal gatherings where Washington met with his officers in uniform. Duvall's Tavern in Alexandria is the first recorded time in which George Washington celebrated in a social setting while back to his civilian life. While people may have referred to him as "General Washington" as a sign of respect, he no longer held an active commission in the Continental army. He was a citizen again.

Since Duvall's Tavern was the first public appearance of George Washington after resigning his commission, it makes the celebration in Alexandria rich with significance. The location of Duvall's Tavern still exists. Visitors can pass it and read that Washington was feted at Duvall's Tavern on December 31, 1783. Additionally, there is a statue of a younger Washington sitting outside the location. In many ways, the location still acts partially as a tavern. Taverns were the equivalent of inns or hotels. The current site of Duvall's Tavern still has lodging, as it is available for rent on Airbnb.

Plaque marking the site of Duvall's Tavern in Alexandria, opened in 1783. George Washington was honored here on December 31, 1783, shortly after resigning his commission. *Photo by the author.*

On December 31, 1783, Alexandrians toasted not only George Washington but also the good fortune of the new nation. America was incorporated under the Articles of Confederation. The work of building the country was about to begin. Washington's first term as president was still six years away. Over that time, significant changes would occur that inspired a new form of government under a new constitution. George Washington and his Alexandria friends took important steps to bring about the transformation.

# Chapter 25

# BUILDING ALEXANDRIA'S INSTITUTIONS

In the post–Revolutionary War period of the mid-1780s, there were many national challenges under the Articles of Confederation. In Alexandria, significant efforts were made to build the new independent nation through local institutions. During this time, George Washington worked with his friends in Alexandria to create and build these institutions. One of the best examples was the Alexandria Academy, founded in 1785. The mission of the academy was to provide a free school for children in Alexandria, including poor and orphaned children.

Washington's friend and fellow Revolutionary War veteran Dr. William Brown helped spearhead the establishment of the Alexandria Academy. In doing so, Brown sought Washington's backing for the new school. In a letter dated November 24, 1785, Washington wrote to Brown, "As far as it is in my power [I] will give [the Alexandria Academy] support."[148] Washington concluded that there is "nothing of more importance than the education of youth." He fulfilled his commitment by pledging £50 annually to the Alexandria Academy.[149] After Washington's death in 1799, his will showed that he left twenty shares of Bank of Alexandria stock, worth $4,000, to the Alexandria Academy.[150]

Washington strengthened the civic health of Alexandria through his involvement in the Freemasons. Organizations like the Freemasons played a critical role in the civic and social institutions of cities like Alexandria. Early in Washington's life, he "was initiated an Entered Apprentice on November 4, 1752," at the Fredericksburg Lodge in Fredericksburg, Virginia.[151] But he was later an active member of the Alexandria

Historical marker for the Alexandria Academy, established in 1785 with the support of George Washington, who served as a trustee. Washington also left twenty shares of Bank of Alexandria stock to the Alexandria Academy. *Photo by the author.*

Freemason lodge. Alexandria's Freemason lodge was chartered on February 3, 1783, as Lodge No. 39. On April 22, 1788, Lodge No. 39 became Alexandria Lodge No. 22 with a charter from the Grand Lodge of Virginia. Simultaneously, Washington agreed to be charter master of Lodge No. 22. Thus began his affiliation with the Alexandria Lodge of Freemasons.

Several of the leading Alexandrians who were involved in the lodge included Robert Adam, who was one of John Carlyle's business partners through the firm Carlyle & Adam. Adam was also a signer of the Fairfax County Resolves. George As the reader will recall, Washington had relied on Adam as one of the merchants who bought his fish from Mount Vernon.

Another prominent Freemason was Dr. Elisha Cullen Dick. Dr. Dick was also a Quaker and played a critical leadership role in Lodge No. 22 as its worshipful master. Lodge No. 22 comprised a strong network of Alexandrians who were committed to the health and well-being of society through the cultivation of virtue and promoting values that made good citizens.

Grave marker of Dr. Elisha Cullen Dick in Alexandria. Dick was one of George Washington's physicians during his final illness in December 1799 and later served as mayor of Alexandria. *Photo by the author.*

As a Freemason, Washington performed Masonic rites at the funeral of his friend William Ramsay in 1785. Ramsay's son, Dennis, was also a Freemason and would perform Masonic rites at George Washington's funeral on December 18, 1799. To this day, Freemasons are proud of "Brother Washington." When Washington was inaugurated at Federal Hall on April 30, 1789, the St. John's Lodge No. 1, Ancient York Masons, provided the Bible that George Washington laid his hands on to take the oath of office.[152] When Washington was inaugurated as president, he was an active Freemason, and his membership was with the Alexandria Lodge No. 22.

George Washington also continued to play an integral role in religious institutions in Alexandria. He was still a member and attended services at Christ Church Episcopal. In fact, just as he had helped finance the church with the purchase of a box pew in 1773, Washington provided economic assistance to the church in the form of "pew rents," which was a subscription service that pew owners paid. These subscriptions were an important source of financing. After the Revolutionary War, the church ended its affiliation with the Church of England. This meant that church and state were separated. Money could no longer be raised through taxing parishioners.

In splitting from the Church of England, the Episcopal Church in America was established. Reverend David Griffith, who was rector of Christ Church from 1780 to 1789, was active in the establishment of the new Episcopal Church. Griffith had been chosen to serve as rector of Christ Church shortly after his service in the American Revolution.

Reverend Griffith remained close to Washington after the war. Washington's pew rent payment was £5 per year. Converting and inflation-adjusting the price to 2025 brings the cost to about $1,300. By 1787, there were seven pew holders, including George Washington. Furthermore, the new vestry authorized subscriptions from other non-pew owners who belonged to the church. The goal was to raise an amount to pay the rector's salary. The amount was not to exceed £150 per year. This would provide a comfortable six-figure salary in today's dollars but would not exceed $250,000 annually.

Reverend Griffith sent a letter to George Washington dated November 3, 1788. In the letter, Reverend Griffith told Washington that he was late on his payment and that his kids needed winter clothing. Reverend Griffith wrote, "Being much in want of Money to furnish my family with the necessary Winter clothing, my Son waits on you for your Pewrent (£5) which was due the 1st day of August last."[153]

George Washington's tardiness in payment notwithstanding, he continued to remain active in the church and attended services until the end of his life.

Washington also backed another religious institution that was created in the 1780s. Washington's former aide-de-camp and business partner John Fitzgerald was one of the few Irish Catholics in Alexandria. Fitzgerald dreamed of establishing a Catholic parish in his hometown. Washington supported Fitzgerald's vision. After having dinner with Fitzgerald at his home in Alexandria on St. Patrick's Day, Washington recorded in his journal that he left £1.50 sterling silver to Fitzgerald for the "German congregation," which was Washington's reference to what would become the Catholic church.[154] With a donation of a half-acre of land from Robert T. Hooe, Fitzgerald successfully established the Catholic parish by 1795.[155] The Basilica of Saint Mary was the first Catholic parish established in Virginia. The parish remains active today and was designated a minor basilica by the Vatican in 2017.[156]

Beyond Washington's victories as a general and his service as president, his private life in Alexandria provides an example of a model citizen. He was active in his community through the promotion of institutions that would allow his friends and neighbors to flourish. This included opportunities for education through the Alexandria Academy. Washington advocated for civic virtue through his membership and support for the Alexandria Freemason Lodge. Finally, George Washington's continued participation and financial backing of churches manifested his understanding that religion inclined man toward a higher purpose through cultivation of the soul.

# Chapter 26

# THE POTOMAC COMPANY

In the first year after the Revolutionary War, George Washington turned fifty-two. He had served in two major wars and had been the leader of one that spanned eight and a half years. One might imagine that he was ready to settle down and enjoy a peaceful life with leisurely pursuits.

But Washington and his Alexandria friends had a country to build. Their ambitions for America were as wide as the Potomac River. Indeed, one can imagine George Washington standing under Mount Vernon's grand piazza, looking across the expanse of the Potomac River specifically with an eye to the west.

Since his teenage years as a surveyor, George Washington acquired significant tracts of land. Throughout his life, the total amount of acreage that he acquired was nearly seventy thousand acres. Much of Washington's land was in the Ohio River Valley. He believed that this acreage had immense value as the fate of America lay in the West. However, during the Revolutionary War, Washington was unable to inspect his land. That was about to change. George Washington was ready to return to his early days of surveying and look west again.

He called on his friend and fellow veteran Dr. James Craik. Craik had joined Washington in prior surveys, including one before the Revolutionary War in 1770. On July 10, 1784, Washington wrote a letter to Craik in which he explained, "I have come to a resolution…to take a trip to the Western Country this Fall, & for that purpose to leave home the first of September."[157]

Dr. Craik joined George Washington in September. They rode west and trekked through the wild and undeveloped wilderness of the new nation. During this time, George Washington studied his tracts of land on the Little Kanawha and Great Kanawha. This land totaled 23,216 acres. He had received it for his service during the French and Indian War as promised by Governor Dinwiddie in 1754.

While surveying was one of the primary purposes of this expedition, there was another benefit. Washington, Craik, and the western frontiersmen whom they encountered discussed opening the Potomac River to interior navigation. Since the earliest time of European settlement, the Potomac River was viewed as a navigable waterway into the interior of America. Alexandria was founded strategically below the fall line of the Potomac River. To continue navigating past Alexandria and farther west was difficult but not impossible. It would take development in the form of locks and canals, which would allow small boats to bypass the Great Falls.

By the time Washington returned to Mount Vernon in October 1784, he was ready to begin the process of working to formally establish a company that could develop the Potomac River for navigation. To build this company, he worked with fellow Revolutionary War veterans from Alexandria, including his former aide-de-camp John Fitzgerald. George Washington's friend, veteran, and Alexandria merchant George Gilpin was also involved in the creation of the Potomac Company.

The company was a promising start-up in early America. It was chartered by legislatures in both Maryland and Virginia. The company was created in Alexandria, and the first meetings were held at Lomax Tavern. George Washington traveled from Mount Vernon to Alexandria to discuss company plans. On May 17, 1785, Washington wrote, "I went to Alexandria to the appointed meeting of the Subscribers to the Potomack Navigation. Upon comparing, & examining the Books of the different Managers, it was found, including the Subscriptions in behalf of the two States, & the 50 Shares which the Assembly of Virginia had directed to be Subscribed for me, (& which I then declared I would only hold in trust for the State) that their were 403 Shares Subscribed, which being more than sufficient to constitute the Company under the Act—the Subscribers proceeded to the choice of a President & 4 Directors; the first of which fell upon me. The votes for the other four fell upon Governors Johnson & Lee of Maryland and Colonels Fitzgerald & Gilpin of this State."[158]

As we can read in Washington's diary, he was allotted fifty shares in the Potomac Company from Virginia. However, he put the shares in trust and,

Great Falls on the Potomac River, a dramatic natural landmark near Washington's Mount Vernon estate. George Washington envisioned the river as a key commercial route. *Photo by the author.*

in his will, specifically left them for the creation of a national university.[159] Washington was also elected president of the Potomac Company. The two directors from Virginia were Gilpin and Fitzgerald.

Washington and the other directors of the Potomac Company worked tirelessly to make the company successful. There are many occasions in which Washington returned to Alexandria for meetings of the Potomac Company. In fact, he often dined at Lomax's tavern during or after the meetings. For example, on January 3, 1787, Washington wrote, "Rid to Alexandria to a meeting of the board of Directors of the Potomack Co. Did the business which occasioned the Meeting. Dined at Lomax's & returned home in the evening."[160]

Nevertheless, the work of the Potomac Company was slow and tedious. There were unexpected costs, weather issues, and labor shortages. The project took seventeen years to complete and was not finished until 1802. Washington never saw the project fully completed. Nevertheless, he never wavered in his support for the project and the company.

The Potomac Company was symbolic of Washington's commitment to America. It was the epitome of a commercial enterprise that also intertwined with political ambitions. The goal was to unite the far-flung reaches of the country into a cohesive system of trade. The Potomac Company was to be part of a giant supply chain. It was the precursor to more successful canals like the Chesapeake and Ohio (C&O), which eventually bought the Potomac Company in 1828. While the Potomac Company did not accomplish what Washington and Alexandrians intended, the Erie Canal in New York became the clearest manifestation of what Washington had dreamed of creating.

New York City became America's commercial powerhouse because of the Erie Canal's success. This is what Washington and Alexandrians rightly

Great Falls, one of the most dramatic places to view the Potomac River. *Photo by the author.*

anticipated might happen to Alexandria. This is why only a few years after the Potomac Company was created, Washington wanted the nation's capital to be situated along the shores of the Potomac River. Furthermore, Washington directed Alexandria to be included within America's capital city with the anticipation that Washington, D.C., might become a thriving commercial capital.

However, several years before the capital was created, the Potomac Company revealed that America faced significant political hurdles. In trying to build the Potomac Company, it became clear that the form of government under the Articles of Confederation had significant limitations. The Virginia law that authorized the creation of the Potomac Company passed the legislature on January 5, 1785.[161] But there were issues to be worked out with the State of Maryland regarding water rights on the Potomac River. This set the stage for a meeting in Alexandria in March 1785. The meeting in Alexandria was the first of several meetings that led directly to America's constitution.

# Chapter 27

# ALEXANDRIA AND THE ROAD TO THE CONSTITUTIONAL CONVENTION

*Alexandria, Virginia*
*March 21, 1785*

Two Virginians were no-shows. They were supposed to meet in Alexandria with four neighbors from across the Potomac River in Maryland. Three (not four) Marylanders arrived on schedule. They were well prepared and eager to settle an important matter of mutual benefit to both states: Which state possessed rights to the Potomac River?

Several of the Marylanders were excited to travel to Virginia with the hopes of seeing George Washington. In fact, one of the Marylanders, Thomas Stone, had jubilantly written to George Washington on January 28, 1785. Stone told Washington that he was going to be in Alexandria in March and that he hoped to visit Washington at Mount Vernon after the important meeting. Stone's letter also explained the details of the meeting as follows:

> *Mr. Jenifer, Johnson, Chase & myself are appointed Commissioners to Settle the Jurisdiction and Navigation of the Bay & the Rivers Potomac & Pocomoke with the Commissioners of Virginia. We have also instructions to make application to Pennsylvania. for leave to clear a Road from Potomac to the Western Waters—Our Assembly propose the Meeting of the Commissioners to be on the 21st of March at Alexandria.*[162]

Thomas Stone was accompanied by Samuel Chase and Major Daniel of St. Thomas Jenifer. Major Jenifer dined with Washington at Mount Vernon on the evening of March 20. He then left for Alexandria on March 21. Although Washington was not one of the appointed commissioners from Virginia, he was supportive of the meeting and planned to track its progress.

Among the bustling taverns in Alexandria, two Virginia commissioners—James Madison and Edmund Randolph—were nowhere to be seen. The Marylanders must have been annoyed. They made the trek across the Potomac River and had been stood up! However, while Madison and Randolph were not there, two other Virginians, George Mason and Alexander Henderson, did arrive to represent the Commonwealth of Virginia. In fact, Washington had sent one of his carriages to give George Mason a ride to Alexandria. Henderson, a wealthy Virginia merchant, was from Prince William County but had a store in Alexandria. Since he had stores in Colchester, Occoquan, and Alexandria, Henderson is known as "father of the American chain store."[163]

Under the Articles of Confederation, each American state acted like a sovereign nation. This is manifested by the fact that each state sent commissioners to negotiate with the other. It displayed the need for a more unified national government that could coordinate issues such as interstate commerce. If all went well at the meeting in Alexandria, it could lay the foundation for further cooperation among states. Washington and the commissioners from Maryland and Virginia hoped that it might also become a model for a national convention.

Despite Madison and Randolph's absence, Mason and Henderson began conversations with the Maryland commissioners. George Washington rode from Mount Vernon to Alexandria on March 22 to check on the conference. When he arrived, Washington learned that the other Virginia commissioners were not there. From the timing of Washington's trip and the subsequent days that followed, it appears likely that there was an agreement to take the meeting from Alexandria to Mount Vernon.

On March 24, Washington wrote, "Sent my Carriage to Alexandria for Colo. Mason according to appointment—who came in about dusk."[164] Washington's mention of an "appointment" is what hints at the agreement to wait and then bring Mason and the other commissioners to Mount Vernon. On the following day, March 25, the three Marylanders and Alexander Henderson arrived at Mount Vernon.

The commissioners enjoyed Washington's hospitality for several days. However, their discussions also included business matters, specifically focusing on the rights to the Potomac River. Finally, on March 28, an

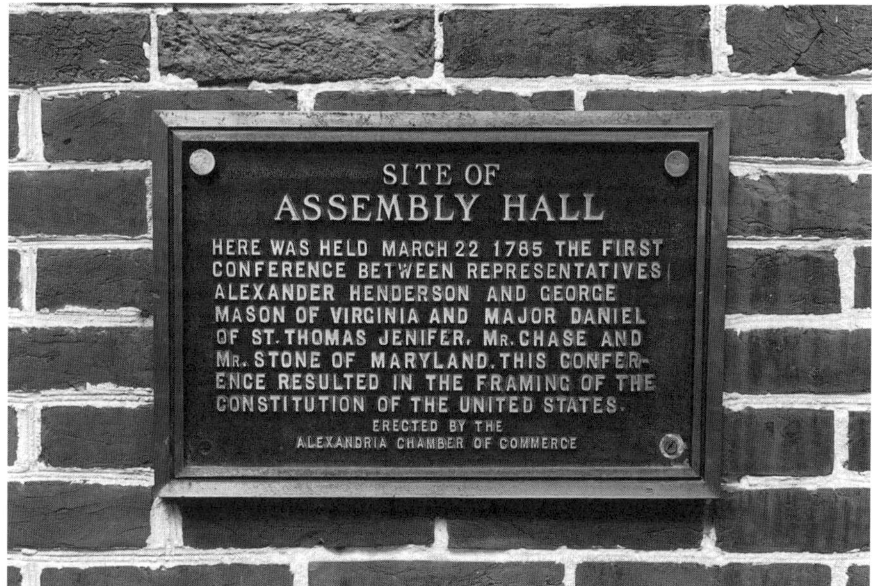


Plaque marking the site of Assembly Hall in Alexandria, where commissioners from Virginia and Maryland met in March 1785 to negotiate water rights on the Potomac River. This meeting laid the groundwork for the Constitutional Convention. *Photo by the author.*

agreement was reached. A total of thirteen clauses defined the waterways as "a common Highway Free for Use and Navigation of any vessel belonging" to Virginia or Maryland.[165] Despite the initial hurdles, compromise was attained, and the commissioners had accomplished their goals. Since the meeting had been moved from Alexandria to Mount Vernon, we know this agreement as the Mount Vernon Compact.

It was the first of its kind in the newly formed confederation of American states. However, it hinted at the need for something more significant. Both the Virginia and Maryland legislatures approved the compact. Momentum grew from events in Alexandria and Mount Vernon. The Mount Vernon Compact set the stage for a meeting in Annapolis, Maryland. The Annapolis Convention began on September 11, 1786. At this convention, the Virginians were on time. In fact, it was James Madison who played an active role in the convention. Surprisingly, at this meeting, the Marylanders did not show up to the convention in their own state!

The meeting in Annapolis was formally called a "Meeting of Commissioners to Remedy Defects of the Federal Government." Unlike the Mount Vernon Conference, there was no formal agreement worked out between the states. On the other hand, something more consequential happened. The Annapolis Convention called on Congress and the states to send representatives to a larger convention. In fact, the follow-on convention was also supposed to address the defects at the heart of the Articles of Confederation. Thus, the Annapolis Convention was the springboard for the convention in Philadelphia to be held in 1787. George Washington enthusiastically supported this step, as he believed that the national government was inefficient and dysfunctional in its current state.

During the time of the Annapolis Convention, another urgent problem stirred in Massachusetts. A former officer in the Continental army, Daniel Shays, led an open rebellion in western Massachusetts. Shays's Rebellion was yet another manifestation of the Article of Confederation's weaknesses. It exposed the government's failure to support veterans and quell internal rebellion. Thus, the stage was set for the Constitutional Convention in 1787, which we will discuss in the "Constitutional Convention and Ratification" chapter.

The road to the Constitutional Convention began in Alexandria, Virginia. When Washington traveled to the city on March 22, he invited the conversations to continue at Mount Vernon. If Washington had not been interested in the meeting, he might not have traveled to check on its progress. Thus, there might have been no Mount Vernon Compact, and the frustrated Marylanders may have gone home complaining about their Virginia neighbors. The meetings, which began in Alexandria and finished at Mount Vernon, provided both the model and inspiration for the Philadelphia Convention that framed America's constitutional form of government.

# Chapter 28

# THE CONSTITUTIONAL CONVENTION

George Washington was shocked to learn of an insurrection led by an embittered Continental army officer, Daniel Shays. Several of Washington's friends, including Henry Lee, communicated with him through letters that emphasized the critical nature of the uprising, which happened in western Massachusetts. In one letter from September 8, 1786, Lee emphasized that Shays's Rebellion necessitated the formation of a stronger national government. Lee wrote to Washington, "The period seems to be fast approaching when the people of these U. States must determine to establish a permanent capable government or submit to the horrors of anarchy and licentiousness."[166] Washington agreed. Change was needed.

Lee's letter to Washington arrived shortly before the Annapolis Convention, which was held September 11–14, 1786. While the Annapolis Convention did not accomplish a "permanent capable government" that Lee and Washington both wanted, it was a "stepping-stone to the Constitutional Convention."[167] At the urging of other Virginians like James Madison, George Washington made the decision to attend the Philadelphia Convention. On May 9, 1787, Washington traveled back to Philadelphia as he had done for the First and Second Continental Congresses in 1774 and 1775, respectively.

On Sunday evening, May 6, Washington had dinner with three friends from Alexandria: Colonel Fitzgerald, Dr. Stuart, and Dr. James Craik.[168] On May 7, another friend and Revolutionary War veteran from Alexandria,

Colonel Simms, came to Mount Vernon and held a business meeting with Washington about the Potomac Company.[169] On May 8, the evening before Washington left for Philadelphia, Charles Lee from Alexandria came to dinner. Charles Lee was the brother of Henry "Light-Horse Harry" Lee. Charles Lee would take up residence at Duvall's Tavern in 1789. He was destined to become the third attorney general of the United States and was appointed to that position by President Washington.

At the Constitutional Convention, George Washington was accompanied by former Alexandria trustee George Mason, who was part of the Virginia Delegation. Washington and Mason traveling together to Philadelphia had echoes from before the Revolutionary War when both men worked together in Alexandria to pass the Fairfax Resolves on July 18, 1774. Thirteen years later, they had a new internal challenge rather than an external enemy. It is also worth noting that Major Daniel of St. Thomas Jenifer attended the Constitutional Convention as one of the Maryland delegates. Major St. Thomas Jenifer was one of the commissioners from Maryland who arrived in Alexandria and worked out the Mount Vernon Compact in 1785. One of the no-show Virginia commissioners, Edmund Randolph, was present as a delegate in Philadelphia. However, rather than being a no-show, Randolph was actually early to the Philadelphia Convention!

The Constitutional Convention began on May 25, 1787. The Virginians were the first delegates to arrive in Philadelphia and presented a unified front and an ambitious plan to remake the government. The delegates in Philadelphia quickly realized that the Virginia Plan was more than a plan to alter and change the form of government. It was proposing an entirely new form of government in which state sovereignty was superseded by a national government.

George Washington's leadership at the Constitutional Convention was critical. He spoke very little. It was his presence as America's most respected leader that gave the convention credibility and popular support. Mason was a more active participant. He sought to influence much of what was included or excluded from the Constitution. When the ink dried on the final form of the Constitution, Mason determined that there was more excluded than included. His principal objection was a lack of Bill of Rights. Thus, he declined to put his signature on the final document. He was one of three delegates who objected to the Constitution and refused to sign, along with Elbridge Gerry of Massachusetts and Edmund Randolph of Virginia. This action caused a rupture in the friendship between George Washington and George Mason. Their friendship was

The flounder house of Charles Simms in Old Town Alexandria. Simms was a Revolutionary War officer, lawyer, and mayor of Alexandria, as well as a friend of George Washington's. *Photo by the author.*

permanently damaged, and Washington and Mason spent little time together and had few correspondences after 1787.

George Washington and Alexandria were very much in favor of the Constitution. Washington shared the same political points of view as the leading citizens of Alexandria. For those who opposed the Constitution like George Mason, they became known as anti-Federalists. By contrast, Washington and most Alexandrians were Federalists. The Alexandrians who saw him depart before the Constitutional Convention—including Fitzgerald, Stuart, Craik, Simms, and Lee—were all Federalists and would be helpful in the political fight that still lay ahead after Philadelphia.

The Constitutional Convention concluded in Philadelphia on September 17, 1787. However, it was now sent to the states for ratification. There were nine states needed. Mason would help lead the charge in Virginia against ratification. Washington would have a lot at stake in the direction Virginia chose to take. In the fall of 1787, Washington and Alexandria prepared for the work of ratifying the Constitution.

# Chapter 29

# RATIFICATION

The delegates whom Alexandria sent to the Virginia Ratifying Convention from June 2 through June 27, 1788, provide the clearest example of Alexandria's Federalist political leanings and unwavering support for George Washington. There were two delegates, Charles Simms and David Stuart, who came from Alexandria and represented the city as delegates from Fairfax County.

Dr. David Stuart was born in Virginia in 1753, but his family were originally from Scotland. Like other Alexandria doctors, he was formally educated at the University of Edinburgh. He also studied medicine in Paris. He returned to Virginia and moved to Alexandria in 1783. After settling in Alexandria, he met and married Eleanor "Nelly" Calvert Custis. Nelly had been married to Martha's son, John "Jacky" Parke Custis, who died after the American victory at Yorktown in 1781.

When Stuart moved to Alexandria and wed Nelly, he quickly became enmeshed in Alexandria society and grew close to Washington. He eventually became a director of the Potomac Company and a trustee of the Alexandria Academy. Furthermore, Stuart represented Alexandria as a Fairfax County member of the Virginia House of Delegates. In this capacity, Washington and Stuart developed a close political bond, with numerous letters between the two men. Even before the ratification convention, Washington relied on Stuart as a political ally and confidant in Richmond. In one notable letter, Stuart wrote to Washington after the Annapolis Convention in 1786 and told him that "amending the articles of confederation" was "important and delicate, but absolutely necessary."[170] Additionally, Stuart told Washington, "From some conversation with Mr. Madison on this business, I have reason to think you will be requested to act on it."[171] As a result, Stuart suggested that Washington was going to be called to serve as president of the Constitutional Convention.

In addition to Stuart, Charles Simms represented Alexandria as a delegate from Fairfax County. Simms was born in Prince William County, Virginia, in 1755 and practiced law in Alexandria. Simms was a distinguished veteran of the American Revolution and had served under Washington's command as a member of Twelfth, Sixth, and Second Virginia Regiments. In fact, he attained the rank of colonel before leaving the service in 1779. Like Stuart, Simms served in the Virginia House of Delegates and represented Fairfax County.

Simms also worked with Washington as a lawyer. On September 22, 1786, Washington wrote Simms a lengthy letter asking him to help settle land disputes related to his holdings on the western frontier. He also asked Simms to find purchasers for some of his "unproductive" lands in Pennsylvania and to assist him with an outstanding debt that was owed to him.[172] Like Stuart, Simms was also involved in the Potomac Company and later became president of the company. He was active in the local Freemason lodge and a member of the vestry at Christ Church. There is a property in between the Carlyle House and Visitor Center that Simms once owned. It is a simple "flounder house," which is distinctive due to its lack of windows on one side, which made people think of the flat or eyeless side of a flounder fish. Simms is currently interred in the burial ground of Christ Church Episcopal.

Washington needed his friends during ratification. He had staked his reputation on the Constitution's adoption by the states. As state conventions began to vote, Washington paid close attention to the progress. Going into the spring of 1788, the issue remained in doubt. Nine states were needed. Several of the states like Virginia and New York had staunch anti-Federalist political factions. Politicians against ratification like George Mason believed that the Constitution was incomplete without a Bill of Rights. Many states ratified the Constitution on the condition that amendments would be added. Nevertheless, Washington opposed the Constitution's detractors. For Washington, the goal was not to "demand perfection" from the document. George Mason saw things differently, and his objections caused a significant fallout not only with his old friend George Washington but also with residents in Alexandria. Mason was also simultaneously entangled in legal disputes with the City of Alexandria.

However, in the days leading up to Virginia's ratification, George Washington's interactions and conversations with neighbors in Alexandria gave him hope for ratification. As an aspiring big city, Alexandria's merchant political class was ardently Federalist. Their support for the new national project helped provide strong backing from a significant portion of Virginia. Additionally, Washington had other allies like Henry "Light-Horse" Harry Lee, who had ties to Alexandria via his family and his own personal investments. Eventually, Henry Lee would settle in Alexandria as a permanent resident. However, in 1788, he represented Westmoreland County, which was the county in which George Washington was born in 1732.

By the time Virginia's convention began on June 2, 1788, eight states had ratified the constitution. If Virginia was the next state to ratify, then the Constitution would be adopted as the new form of government. However, formidable opponents of the Constitution included Richard Henry Lee and Patrick Henry. They came out hard against ratification. Richard Henry Lee was from another branch of the vast Lee family dynasty. He was a second cousin to Henry Lee. The two diverged significantly in their political opinions. While Henry Lee was a friend, confidant, and loyal supporter of Washington, as previously discussed, Richard Henry Lee was suspected of being involved in the Conway Cabal.

Patrick Henry used his oratorical skills to urge delegates to oppose the Constitution. In the same way he mustered colonial support against the Stamp Act in 1765, Henry sought to prevent the Constitution's passage for fear that a national government stripped power that should be held by each state. Furthermore, Henry had inspired his Virginians with his rousing "Give me liberty or give me death" speech in 1775. He channeled the same rhetorical energy into speeches against ratification in June 1788.

Thus, Alexandria's representatives, Dr. Stuart and Charles Simms, had strong competition when they arrived in Richmond in June 1788 for the ratifying convention. Stuart specifically reprised his role as Washington's eyes and ears in Richmond, just as he had during sessions in the Virginia General Assembly. While Washington was not physically present in Richmond, Stuart, Simms, and Henry Lee functioned in a surrogate role for him.

Washington's presence loomed large over the convention. Biographer Ron Chernow writes, "Washington moved stealthily in the background of the ratification process." There is only one way that this could be accomplished, and it was through his political allies who were present in Richmond. People who knew him and were close to him could convey Washington's thoughts and feelings. Washington and Stuart wrote several letters to

Grave of Charles Simms at Christ Church in Alexandria. Simms was a Revolutionary War officer, lawyer, and mayor of Alexandria, as well as a friend of George Washington's. *Photo by the author.*

each other as the convention progressed. In one letter, Washington spoke about the Constitution's adoption as being "auspicious for the happiness of this Country."[173] In another letter, Washington wrote to Stuart, "I hope the good sense of the Country will be superior to, and overcome the local views of some, and the arrogant and malignant pride of others."[174]

Despite the strong opposition from Mason, Henry, and Richard Henry Lee, Virginians like James Madison made strong, impassioned appeals for the Constitution's ratification. Between Madison's stellar leadership and Washington's Alexandria friends making his influence felt, ratification passed with eighty-nine votes in support to seventy-nine in opposition. A ten-vote margin, but enough to officially become the tenth state to ratify. Unfortunately for Virginia, New Hampshire claimed the spot as the critical ninth state. Nevertheless, Virginia's ratification was significant because it was George Washington's home state. It was important for him personally to ensure that his state was part of the new constitutional republic. Furthermore, the discussions quickly turned toward who would serve as president. With Virginia's ratification, George Washington became a leading candidate for the role of America's chief executive.

However, there was time to celebrate first. With the adoption of the Constitution, the celebrations kicked off up and down the Potomac River. When news reached Alexandria, the city "blazed with lights in celebration" accompanied by "discharges of cannon."[175] On June 28, 1788, Washington wrote, "The Inhabitants of Alexandria having received the News of the ratification of the proposed Constitution by this State, and that of New Hampshire and having determined on public rejoicings, part of which to be in a dinner, to which this family was invited Colo. Humphreys my Nephew G.A. Washington & myself went up to it and returned in the afternoon."[176]

Washington gathered with his Alexandria friends at John Wise's Tavern on the corner of Cameron and North Fairfax Streets. The building was built before 1777 by John Dalton, Washington's friend, who passed away in the same year. In a letter to Charles Cotesworth Pinckney, Washington reported, "The Citizens of Alexandria, when convened, constituted the first public company in America, which had the pleasure of pouring libation to the prosperity of the ten States that had actually adopted the general government."[177]

Wise's Tavern in Old Town Alexandria, where George Washington made his first public appearance after being elected president in April 1789. *Photo by the author.*

Thus, on June 28, 1788, for the first time in America, glasses were raised in a toast to the new country. Cannon shells exploded over the Potomac River, punctuating the sky with a martial spirit. The Articles of Confederation had been a bridge, seeing the nation through a period of postwar transition. It is appropriate that Alexandria held one of the first celebrations of the ratified Constitution. Washington and his Alexandria friends were among the first people to recognize the Articles of Confederation's defects. They took steps to mitigate those shortcomings as early as March 22, 1785. The political fight for a new government was quicker than the eight-and-a-half-year war for independence. By the anniversary of July 4, 1788, America was officially a republic with a new constitution. By the following year, America would have its first president.

# Chapter 30

# CALLED BACK TO SERVICE

On April 14, 1789, a representative from Congress, Charles Thompson, rode to Mount Vernon with an important message. His Excellency General Washington was unanimously elected president of the new constitutional republic. Once again, Washington's country called him into service, as it had in 1775 and 1787. Washington wasted little time preparing to make the trip from Mount Vernon to New York City, which was the first seat of America's government and the site of Washington's inauguration on April 30, 1789.

The journey to New York took eight days, with stops along the way to meet and greet grateful citizens in cities like Baltimore and Philadelphia. However, the first city on Washington's journey was Alexandria. Washington was escorted into Alexandria to a celebration at John Wise's Tavern. It was the same tavern in which he celebrated Virginia's ratification of the Constitution less than one year prior.

By 1789, many of the first generation of Alexandria's founders were now deceased, including John Dalton (died 1777), John Carlyle (died 1780), and William Ramsay (died 1785). When William Ramsay died, George Washington marched in his funeral procession performing Masonic rites. Washington and Ramsay had been friends for years, and they had both helped each other during critical periods in each other's lives. This fact was not lost on William Ramsay's son, Dennis Ramsay.

Dennis Ramsay was the mayor of Alexandria when George Washington was elected president. As mayor, he presided over the gathering at Wise's

Tavern on the evening of April 16, 1789. This was George Washington's first public appearance outside of Mount Vernon since being informed of his election as president. When Alexandria's mayor, Dennis Ramsay, raised his glass and toasted Washington, he had the distinction of being the first public official to greet George Washington as president of the United States at a public gathering. As a result, the city of Alexandria was the first city that George Washington was publicly addressed as president. This was more than appropriate considering that Washington's early political career began in Alexandria as a member of the House of Burgesses representing Fairfax County from 1765 to 1775 and as a town trustee, beginning in 1763.

Dennis Ramsay's speech did not flatter Washington with heaps of praise. In fact, it was humble in tone. Ramsay's speech spoke about the special bond between Washington and Alexandria. His speech illustrated how since Alexandria's founding in 1749, both Washington and Alexandria had benefited and mutually supported each other. Their destinies had been intertwined. Ramsay explained further that Alexandria appreciated Washington not strictly because of his credentials as commander-in-chief and Washington's battlefield victories. Instead, it was in mundane matters such as Washington's business relationships and his support for education. It was in the ambition of both Washington and the town to build the Potomac River into a suitable waterway for navigation. It was in the way that Washington treated his neighbors as dear friends. Dennis Ramsay knew, for example, that George Washington had paid for his brother's education to Princeton without any desire to be repaid. It was an act of selfless generosity and one that spoke to a strong friendship that Washington shared with Dennis's father, William Ramsay.

George Washington returned the sentiments of Dennis Ramsay and the citizens of Alexandria. There was a note of melancholy in Washington's response as he told the assembly, "Those who have known me best (and you, my fellow citizens, are from your situation, in that number) know better than any others my love of retirement is so great, that no earthly consideration, short of a conviction of duty, could have prevailed upon me to depart."[178]

Furthermore, Washington did not feel the need to convince his fellow citizens of Alexandria that he was going to represent their interests as president. He told them that his "past actions" would "be the pledge of my future conduct."[179] Washington remarked that the words of Ramsay, speaking for the City of Alexandria, offered "tender proof of your friendship."[180] Finally, Washington concluded solemnly, "From an aching heart, I bid you all, my affectionate friends, and kind neighbors, farewell!"[181]

Plaque marking Wise's Tavern in Alexandria, where George Washington made his first public appearance after being elected president in April 1789. *Photo by the author.*

Washington's friends in Alexandria had done much to support him throughout his public and private life. Even in the moment when he departed for New York, the trip itself would not have happened without the assistance of a former mayor of Alexandria, Richard Conway (no direct relation to Thomas Conway from the Conway Cabal). In fact, it was the same Conway who was mayor during Washington's return to Alexandria on December 31, 1783. Conway was the mayor who led toasts to celebrate the end of the Revolutionary War with Washington at Duvall's Tavern on New Year's Eve. Nearly six years later, Washington called on Conway for a favor.

On March 4, 1789, Washington was in a cash crunch. On that date, he wrote a letter to Conway in which he confessed his "want of money."[182] Washington noted the lack of funds was due to a poor crop yield at Mount Vernon and an undervaluing of "Land, which I have offered for Sale."[183] As a result, Washington confessed, "I am inclined to do what I never expected to be reduced to the necessity of doing—that is, to borrow money upon interest."[184]

Initially, Washington requested £500. Two days later, Washington wrote a follow-up letter to Conway thanking him for his "assurance of Money."[185] Washington was relieved that he was able to get a loan from Conway, and he found that the interest rate of 6 percent was satisfactory. He was also conscious of his "journey to New York" and requested an additional £100 to bring the total amount to £600.[186] From George Washington's actual accounting records, the amount ended up being £625 in Maryland currency. Washington paid back the debt in full and with interest on December 15, 1790.[187]

George Washington's need for cash was nothing new. While he was wealthy in terms of assets like land, the assets did not always mean there was cash on hand. But Conway's willingness to provide George Washington with a loan speaks to his faith and trust in Washington and his respect for him as a friend and neighbor. Conway must have agreed without hesitation as evidence by the timing of both Washington's first letter and his follow-up letter. Furthermore, the fact that Conway was willing to accommodate Washington's request for another one hundred pounds shows the measure of esteem in which he held George Washington.

If one were to convert £625 pounds into present dollars, the amount is around $158,000. No small sum of money! Washington's biographers have often drawn the conclusion that this speaks to his dismal financial state less than two months before Washington's inauguration. The fact that America's first president was cash strapped and needed a loan seems like a quirky bit of Washington history. However, the story speaks volumes about Washington's reliance on his network of friends in Alexandria. Richard Conway, as mayor, gave Washington a hero's welcome on December 31, 1783, at Duvall's Tavern. Now, as Washington was preparing to leave to serve as president of the United States, Conway and Alexandria were sending Washington off with his financial affairs in order. As a result, when Washington left Alexandria on April 17, 1789, his Alexandria friends provided him with confidence, assurance, and a fond farewell to serve his country as president.

# Chapter 31

# PRESIDENT WASHINGTON

After George Washington was sworn in as president of the United States, there was no shortage of challenges facing America. On the domestic front, some of the most vexing issues included high debts from the Revolutionary War. In terms of national defense, Britain lingered across the border and maintained fortifications in Canada. Furthermore, there was no sign that American settlers would stop pushing farther west and, in doing so, antagonize numerous Indian tribes. On the foreign policy front, France was on the brink of revolution. Less than three months into Washington's first term, the Bastille prison in Paris would fall into the hands of French revolutionaries. The next decade saw the European continent embroiled in conflict. To manage all these affairs, Washington assembled a cabinet that consisted of Thomas Jefferson as secretary of state, Alexander Hamilton as secretary of the treasury, Henry Knox as secretary of war, and Edmund Randolph as attorney general. It was an impressive team but one that would splinter due to conflicting visions of America.

## A New Financial System and a New Capital City

The first issue that Washington's presidency tackled was that of state debts from the Revolutionary War. As secretary of the treasury, Hamilton designed a plan to fix this problem while simultaneously establishing an entirely new financial system. Hamilton wanted to consolidate state debts under the federal government. But there was resistance to this plan. Jefferson led the opposition and was aided by James Madison. To allow Hamilton's scheme to move forward, the two Virginians needed something in return. What they negotiated was the relocation of the U.S. capital to the south.

The Compromise of 1790 meant that the capital, which was named the District of Columbia, was going to move to a new permanent seat along the Potomac River. The Residence Act passed Congress on July 16, 1790, while the capital was still in New York City. However, the Residence Act stipulated the creation of a new ten-mile-square federal district that would serve as the permanent seat of the U.S. government. In conjunction with this act was the Funding Act of 1790, which Congress passed on August 4, 1790. This act allowed the federal government to assume all state debts from the Revolutionary War.

With the passage of the Residence Act, George Washington strongly influenced the plan for the new seat of government. Washington's dream was to see the Potomac River as a major trade artery linking western states and territories with national and international markets. His involvement in the Potomac Company embodied that vision. By moving the U.S. capital to the shores of the Potomac River, this dream moved one step closer to becoming a reality. With Virginia giving up a portion of its territory, Washington specifically directed Alexandria to be included in the seat of government.

On January 24, 1791, George Washington made a proclamation to the U.S. Senate and House of Representatives. In the proclamation, Washington stated that on December 23, 1788, Maryland had agreed "to cede to Congress a District of ten miles square in this State, for the seat of the government of the United States." On December 3, 1789, the General Assembly of Virginia voted to cede territory as well. The overall land mass was not to exceed "ten miles square"—a total area of one hundred miles. When the district was laid out, Maryland contributed the most territory with sixty-nine miles. Virginia contributed thirty-one miles of land. Looking from north to south, the federal district looks like a diamond, with the Potomac River slicing through the southwest corner of it as a natural barrier between the sides of Virginia and Maryland.

In the proclamation, George Washington specifically declared that the beginning of the four lines should be oriented off "the Court House in Alexandria." The first line would stretch due southwest one half of a mile, and then the other line would stretch due southeast one half of a mile. This would then be the point "to fix the beginning of the said four lines." Washington was acting as surveyor again, just as he had learned the trade in Alexandria as early as 1748. He was now anchoring the base of the federal district in Alexandria. Washington also retained the authorization to appoint commissioners to survey the boundary of the ten-mile-square capital.[188]

After George Washington's proclamation, two of his Alexandria friends, George Gilpin and William Hunter Jr., who was a former mayor and local shipbuilder, began surveying the first lines on their own initiative. George Washington replied to Gilpin and Hunter with gratitude for their work. However, he explained that he had "engaged Mr. Ellicott to make the survey." Andrew Ellicott became the lead surveyor of the federal district. Washington explained to his friends that Ellicott was "one of the most scientific characters we have." But he still hoped that Gilpin and Hunter would assist him and wrote, "I persuade myself that no aids [Ellicott] may want will be withheld by the corporation of Alexandria."[189]

While Washington appointed Andrew Ellicott as the lead surveyor, he also appointed three commissioners to supervise the survey. One of the appointed commissioners was an Alexandrian. In fact, Washington called on his friend and political ally Dr. David Stuart to serve as one of the three commissioners. After the January proclamation in which Washington directed Alexandria to be included in the capital city, Congress passed an amendment to the act with the boundaries approved on March 3, 1791. In the following month, on April 15, Dr. Stuart and many leading citizens of Alexandria gathered half a mile south of the courthouse in the heart of Alexandria. They were present for and witnessed the placement of the first boundary stone of the new capital. The stone was placed on a small piece of land surrounded by marshland where Great Hunting Creek feeds into the Potomac River. In placing the boundary stone, Alexandria was now the foundation from which Washington, D.C., was created. The boundary stone still stands to this day at Jones Point.

Two and half years after the laying of the first boundary stone of the capital city, the boundary stone of the Capitol was laid on September 18, 1793. While the boundary stone of the capital city was in Alexandria, the boundary stone of the U.S. Capitol, which was the location where Congress would physically meet, was across the Potomac River. Nevertheless, on the day of the cornerstone laying, Washington was greeted by "a fife and drum corps from Alexandria."[190] Additionally, the "grand parade to the Capitol site proceeded under the auspices of Lodge No. 22 from Alexandria."[191]

Since the Alexandria Freemason Lodge No. 22 attended the laying of the cornerstone, many of Washington's friends from Alexandria were present, including Dr. Elisha Cullen Dick, who was worshipful master of Alexandria Lodge No. 22. In fact, Dr. Dick was present at the laying of the cornerstone for both the capital city (1791) and the Capitol (1793). Dr. Dick was a well-respected citizen in Alexandria and would later be mayor. As we will see, he was one of the three physicians who attended to George Washington at his deathbed.

As part of the ceremony, an engraved metal plate was placed in the ground, and the cornerstone was laid on top of it. The engraving on the plate specifically mentions Alexandria and reads as follows:

> *This South East corner stone, of the Capitol of the United States of America in the City of Washington, was laid on the 18th day of September, in the thirteenth year of American Independence, in the first year of the second term of the Presidency of George Washington, whose virtues in the civil administration of his country have been as conspicuous and beneficial, as his Military valor and prudence have been useful in establishing her liberties, and in the year of Masonry 5793, by the Grand Lodge of Maryland, several lodges under its jurisdiction, and Lodge 22, from Alexandria, Virginia.*[192]

## War, Neutrality, Banks, and a Divided Cabinet

The Compromise of 1790 was a temporary truce between Hamilton and Jefferson. But the peace did not last. Much of Washington's first term included internal squabbles within his own cabinet. The rivalry between his secretary of state, Jefferson, and secretary of the treasury, Hamilton, grew more intense.

The French Revolution was a flashpoint not only on the world stage but also within America. It entrenched deep divisions between those like Jefferson, who thought that the United States should back the revolutionaries, and Hamilton, who did not want America involved in France's revolution. Many Americans agreed with Jefferson that the United States had a duty to support France in its attempts to overthrow a monarchy. Washington may have been inclined toward this position at the outset, especially when his friend, the Marquis de Lafayette, sent him a seven-inch iron key to the

Bastille prison, which had been seized by French revolutionaries on July 14, 1789. This key, a gift from Lafayette, still hangs in the front hall of Mount Vernon to this day.

Not long after the fall of the Bastille, Washington, Hamilton, and other Federalists began to see sinister signs in the French Revolution. There was a radical wing under the Jacobins that sought to purge France of all monarchical elements as well as the established Catholic Church. As the French Revolution took a more violent turn, European nations sought to contain the revolutionary fervor and prevent it from spreading. On April 20, 1792, the French Legislative Assembly declared war on Austria, which had mobilized troops along their border with France. Prussia quickly entered the war. Great Britain and Russia soon followed. For the remainder of the 1790s, Europe was consumed by constant fighting.

The French Revolution significantly influenced the politics of America. The question for Washington's administration was how America should navigate this bloody period. That answer became obvious on January 21, 1793, when King Louis XVI, who had provided aid and support to America's war for independence, was beheaded before "a crowd of twenty thousand people intoxicated with a lust for revenge."[193] America would not intervene on the side of the French revolutionaries, but neither would it support the European monarchies. America would stay neutral.

On April 22, 1793, America formally declared neutrality with a proclamation that read, "Whereas it appears that a state of war exists between Austria, Prussia, Sardinia, Great-Britain, and the United Netherlands, of the one part, and France on the other, and the duty and interest of the United States require, that they should with sincerity and good faith adopt and pursue a conduct friendly and impartial toward the belligerent powers."[194] The key phrase was "impartial toward the belligerent powers." Alexandria welcomed George Washington's Neutrality Proclamation. The political leanings of Alexandria were strongly Federalist. In theory, neutrality meant that trade and commerce could take place between all countries without consequence. However, the practical reality of this policy was not so simple.

Nevertheless, the City of Alexandria sent Washington a letter that praised the policy. Furthermore, Alexandria invited Washington to celebrate Independence Day on July 4, 1793, at a newly expanded tavern on Cameron and North Royal Street. On Independence Day, the citizens of Alexandria formally praised Washington's "wisdom" by declaring "that America should remain in peace and enjoy the blessings of their free government undisturbed by European concerns."[195] George Washington

*Left*: The ballroom of Gadsby's Tavern in Alexandria, a gathering place for prominent figures, including George Washington and Thomas Jefferson. *Photo by the author.*

*Opposite*: Duvall's Tavern in Alexandria, which opened in 1783 and was later converted into the home of Charles Lee, U.S. attorney general under Washington and John Adams. In 1793, it became the Bank of Alexandria. *Photo by the author.*

replied cordially and affirmed that there were "important advantages, which the United States will experience by remaining in peace."[196] He added, "It remains for the citizens of the United States, to shew to the world, that the reproach heretofore cast on Republican Governments for their want of stability, is without foundation, when that Government is the deliberate choice of an enlightened people."[197] This addendum shows that Washington believed America could be a model to the world that republican government was possible and did not need to devolve into lawlessness and anarchy as it had in France.

Washington's celebration in Alexandria on July 4, 1793, took place at a critical moment in American history. While he was steering the country in a neutral path with respect to Europe, the country was splintering along factional lines. By the end of 1793, Thomas Jefferson had formally resigned as Washington's secretary of state. The Jefferson and Hamilton division had reached a tipping point not only over foreign affairs but also over domestic policy.

In fact, evidence of that policy could be seen in Alexandria in 1793. The former location of Duvall's Tavern and former home of Charles Lee was now the location of the Bank of Alexandria. This was the first chartered bank in Virginia and the second bank chartered south of Philadelphia. On February 25, 1791, Congress authorized the charter for the First Bank of the United States. Like Great Britain, America would have a national bank. It was exactly what Hamilton wanted when he struck a compromise between Jefferson and Madison over the location of the capital city.

With the creation of the new national bank, several branch banks were established in Boston, New York, Charleston, and Baltimore in 1792. In response, the Virginia General Assembly voted on a charter for a bank to

ensure that Virginia did not fall behind the other states. Thus, on November 23, 1792, the Virginia General Assembly voted to incorporate the Bank of Alexandria.[198] Shares in the Bank of Alexandria were sold on December 7, 1792, in what can be considered one of America's earliest initial public offerings (IPOs). Bank stockholders met and elected directors of the bank, which included many of George Washington's friends and business associates such as Richard Conway, William Hartshorne, Robert T. Hooe, and, eventually, John Fitzgerald. On April 9, 1793, two weeks before the Neutrality Proclamation, the Bank of Alexandria formally opened for business.

When George Washington celebrated America's birthday in Alexandria on July 4, 1793, the city of Alexandria epitomized how Federalist policies were ascendant in the United States. There was a new financial system accompanied by a neutral stance toward the wars in Europe. These policies may have been celebrated in Alexandria, but Jeffersonians detested the direction they saw America heading. Jefferson would work to build an opposition party. This opposition would drive a significant wedge between Washington and Jefferson that would not be reconciled when Washington died in December 1799.

## The Whiskey Rebellion

After Jefferson left Washington's cabinet, tension persisted as he and James Madison worked to build a rival political party to oppose Federalist policies. In 1794, Supreme Court Justice John Jay was also sent to Britain to negotiate a treaty that the United States signed with Great Britain and is known as the Jay Treaty. Opponents of the treaty labeled Federalists like Hamilton as "monarchists." Republican papers became increasingly critical of Washington. Far from being a halcyon decade of political unity, the 1790s was quickly showing American politics to be particularly vicious and filled with as much backbiting and political intrigue as any other governmental system.

Much of the political opposition was formed from groups known as the "Democratic Societies." Federalists like Washington saw these organizations as being more than a political threat—they saw them as borderline treasonous and stoking rebellion. In the summer of 1794, America was faced with an internal threat of rebellion in western Pennsylvania. It was an event known as the Whiskey Rebellion, and its principal cause dated to January 1791, when the federal government implemented an excise tax "upon spirits distilled within the United States."[199] Three years later, the protests turned violent specifically when the home of John Neville, a regional tax collector, was deliberately set on fire and destroyed.

Washington called up state militias and organized a force that comprised nearly thirteen thousand soldiers. He placed his friend Henry "Light-Horse Harry" Lee in command of the army. Lee held the rank of major general. Washington and Lee kept in continual contact during the summer and into the fall. In one letter, Washington told Lee, "I consider this insurrection as the first *formidable* fruit of the Democratic Societies."[200] Washington further explained, "That these societies were instituted by the *artful* & *designing* members…primarily to sow the Seeds of Jealousy & distrust among the people, of the government, by destroying all confidence in the Administration of it."[201] Even further in the letter, Washington addressed claims that Jefferson was making about him possibly being under British influence. Washington said to Lee that he could not believe Jefferson would have made an accusation "unless (which I do not believe) he has set me down as one of the most deceitful, & uncandid men living."[202] Washington's letter to Lee shows him confiding in his friend his thoughts on the politics of the day and the source of internal struggle in the United States. It also highlights the division that grew between Washington and Jefferson since Jefferson left Washington's cabinet the year prior.

Nevertheless, Lee did his duty effectively. He mobilized the thirteen-thousand-man army and moved them into western Pennsylvania. As president, Washington also rode into the field as far as Carlisle, Pennsylvania. The mobilization of the militias into a large army was enough to cause a show of force that led to the capitulation of the insurrection. The rebellion ended without a shot being fired. Two of the primary organizers were John Mitchell and Philip Weigel, who were found guilty of treason. However, President Washington pardoned both men.[203]

## Presidential Appointments

Washington's reliance on Henry Lee illustrates his relationship with the Lee family, many of whom lived in Alexandria. By the 1790s, part of the Lee family who were descended from Henry Lee II were well established in Alexandria. After the death of the second attorney general of the United States, William Bradford, George Washington selected Charles Lee as his third attorney general of the United States. Charles Lee lived and practiced law in Alexandria. In fact, he had lived for four years at what was formerly Duvall's Tavern and then became the Bank of Alexandria. It is also worth noting that before Charles Lee lived in the home, the house was occupied by Daniel Roberdeau, who lived there temporarily while building a grand, Federal-style home on South Lee Street (then Water Street).

Before being selected as attorney general, Lee had served for four years from 1789 to 1793 as inspector of customs for the Port of Alexandria. He held this role until he succeeded Charles Simms in the Virginia House of Delegates and represented Fairfax County, which still encompassed Alexandria. However, during his term in the Virginia General Assembly, the Senate confirmed Lee as attorney general, and he assumed office on December 10, 1795. He retained the office through President Adams's administration.

After Adams left office, he made a series of judicial appointments that the incoming Jefferson administration refused to recognize. This triggered what became the foundational Supreme Court case of *Marbury v. Madison*. The case established the process of the Supreme Court's judicial review and is the most important Supreme Court case in U.S. history. With his ruling in *Marbury v. Madison*, Chief Justice John Marshall effectively established the Supreme Court's legitimacy as an equal third branch of government with Congress and the chief executive. Charles Lee represented the plaintiffs in the case, which included William Marbury of Georgetown along with three plaintiffs from Alexandria: Robert T. Hooe, Dennis Ramsay, and William Harper.

Before Washington selected Charles Lee as attorney general, he also sought the brilliant legal mind of his former lawyer, aide-de-camp, and military secretary Robert Harrison, whom he wanted to be an associate justice to the U.S. Supreme Court. Biographer Douglas Freeman wrote that Washington "made particular appeals" to the "beloved 'old Colonel' of Washington's military staff."[204] However, Harrison's health was failing him, and he was physically unable to fill the role. On February 3, 1790, Dr. Craik wrote to Washington about Harrison's "ill state of health" being the reason he could not serve as associate justice. Harrison died on April 2, 1790.

The story exemplifies the extent to which Washington looked to his Alexandria network for support. Not only did Washington want Harrison to serve as an associate justice, but it is also an example of how Dr. Craik cared for many of Washington's friends in Alexandria. Furthermore, Craik also cared for employees and enslaved workers at Mount Vernon. Thus, we see how Washington's friend and physician continued his important work of service even while they were apart. Nevertheless, Washington did enlist the help of Craik's son, George Washington Craik, to work for him in his second term. Craik's son, who was named after George Washington, became President Washington's secretary in 1796.

Throughout Washington's presidency, many of his Alexandria friends wrote to him either looking to help in his administration or to advocate for personnel who could fill key positions. George Washington leaned on his network to fill important positions. As a final example, on April 13, 1793, Washington appointed his former aide-de-camp John Fitzgerald to be collector of customs for the Port of Alexandria.[205] Fitzgerald took the role after Charles Lee's election to the Virginia House of Delegates. In this role, Fitzgerald served directly under Secretary of the Treasury Alexander Hamilton.[206]

# Chapter 32

# A FARM MANAGER AND A SECRETARY

During the time of George Washington's presidency, there were several important people in his life who played critical roles in his personal and professional affairs. The first was Washington's "favored nephew," George Augustine Washington. Born around 1759, George Augustine was originally from Fredericksburg, Virginia, and later served in the Revolutionary War. While nephew Washington was never formally an aide-de-camp to his uncle, he did receive a Congressional appointment as "Ensign in the second Regiment of Virginia" and appears to have done clerical work for his uncle General Washington at Morristown, New Jersey, from 1779 to 1780. Furthermore, George Augustine "was mentioned in a letter dated August 2, 1780, as being an aide-camp to the marquis de Lafayette."[207]

After the Revolutionary War, George Augustine Washington married Martha Washington's favorite niece, Fanny Bassett. The wedding took place at Mount Vernon on October 15, 1785. In the same year, George Washington's distant cousin, Lund Washington, decided to resign from his role as Mount Vernon farm manager. Lund Washington had successfully managed Mount Vernon for two decades. His departure left a big hole, but one that was quickly filled by George Augustine Washington.

As Mount Vernon's farm manager from 1786 until his death from consumption in 1793, George Augustine helped manage the property while Washington was in Philadelphia for the Constitutional Convention (1787) and during his uncle's first term as president (1789–93). Knowing that Mount Vernon was in capable hands allowed Washington to serve his country during the critical transition period from the Articles of Confederation to constitutional republic. George Augustine Washington's specific connections to Alexandria were solidified by a house that he and Fanny purchased on 501 Duke Street. The house still stands to this day.

After George Augustine's death in 1793, Fanny Bassett married Washington's secretary, Tobias Lear. Lear was one of the most important people in the latter part of Washington's life. Born in 1762, Lear was originally from New Hampshire and went to Harvard College. One of Washington's former generals, Benjamin Lincoln, introduced Lear to the Washingtons, and he first worked as a tutor for Martha's grandchildren. However, he soon became George Washington's personal secretary. He served in that role from 1786 and throughout Washington's first term as president. In the same year that George Augustine died, Lear took a temporary break from his job as Washington's secretary. However, he went into business as both a land speculator and a director in the Potomac Company. As a result, he remained professionally close to George Washington. The two maintained a correspondence, as Lear lived in Georgetown.

After Lear married Fanny Bassett on August 6, 1795, the two newlyweds must have spent some time at the same house at 501 Duke Street. One month after their wedding, George Washington noted on September 25, 1795, "Went to Alexandria. Dined with Mr. & Mrs. Lear."[208] Unfortunately for Tobias Lear, Fanny Bassett, who was his second wife, died one year later from tuberculosis. Lear eventually moved to the Mount Vernon plantation and lived at a home called Collingwood, which was on Washington's River Farm. The property was approximately four miles south of Alexandria. Most of Washington's River Farm property now consists of private neighborhoods as well as the American Horticultural Society. Lear's Collingwood home was sadly torn down in the twentieth century. Nevertheless, residents of the area where Lear lived have an Alexandria address despite technically being in Fairfax County.

Home in Alexandria connected to Fanny Bassett Washington and her husband, George Augustine Washington, nephew of George Washington and manager of Mount Vernon. *Photo by the author.*

Lear had significant business dealings in Alexandria on George Washington's behalf.

In 1793, the Bank of Alexandria was fully operational as the first chartered bank in Virginia. Lear helped George Washington buy shares of stock in the bank. In a series of letters in the spring of 1795, Washington authorized Lear to purchase Bank of Alexandria stock. Lear's letter dated May 20, 1795, informed Washington that shares in the Bank of Alexandria could be purchased at $200 each. The shares paid a dividend every six months at an annualized rate of 9 to 10 percent of par value. Washington liked the prospect of the dividend and directed Lear to move forward with the purchase.

Another important financial matter in late 1795 involved Washington's townhouse on Cameron Street. Washington was concerned that he would not be able to rent the townhouse in time for the winter and that it might be "left unoccupied" and suffer damage.[209] As a result, on November 30, 1795, Washington wrote Lear, "If I cannot get a full rent for my house in Alexandria I must be content with what it will fetch."[210]

However, on December 14, 1795, Lear wrote to Washington that he had secured a tenant in the house as of November 17. Lear's letter explained, "I have the pleasure to inform you that your House in Alexandria is rented for sixty pounds Virga Curry per Annum, to Mr Nathl Washington, who will go into it immediately."[211]

Lear and Washington also discussed another offer to buy Washington's half-acre lot on the northwest corner of Prince and South Pitt Streets. On March 21, 1796, Washington wrote to Lear, "A Mr Summers of Alexandria, is very desirous of purchasing my vacant lot in that Town, and having been told that nothing short of a high price would induce me to sell it."[212] He asked Lear to find out if the price being offered was right to sell. Washington added, "I have no wish to part with the lot unless I can do it upon advantageous terms."[213] He also mentioned having thoughts of building on the lot but thought it would be "a good deal of imposition" and that the cost of "workmens wages and materials are very high at this time."[214] Washington held on to the property and did not sell or build on it.

During the period from 1795 to March 1796, much of Washington and Lear's correspondence involved the business of the Potomac Company. Washington never lost interest in the company that he helped start more than a decade prior in Alexandria. However, the letters turned to personal tragedy when Lear informed Washington, "The partner of my life is no more!"[215] Fanny Bassett died of tuberculosis on March 25, 1796. Washington replied from Philadelphia on March 30, "To say how much we loved, and esteemed our departed friend, is unnecessary—She is now no more! but she must be happy, because her virtue has a claim to it."[216] In the same letter, he also invited Lear to come live with him in Philadelphia, saying that there was room for him and "we shall be glad of your company."[217] However, despite Washington's invitation, Lear stayed put in Georgetown.

George Augustine Washington and Tobias Lear were both important to George Washington in the post–Revolutionary War period of his life. Through their respective marriages to Fanny Bassett, they both lived albeit briefly in Alexandria on 501 Duke Street. However, their respective management of Washington's farms and business interests closely interwove them into Alexandria. Lear continued to serve George Washington after Washington's return to Mount Vernon in March 1797. Upon Washington's return, Lear went back to work as Washington's secretary. In this role, he maintained and expanded personal and professional relationships with citizens of Alexandria, which became especially important in the days following Washington's death in December 1799.

# Chapter 33

# RETURNING HOME

On March 20, 1797, Alexandria Mayor Francis Peyton Jr. wrote a letter to Washington that said, "I am directed by the Council of this Town, to solicit the honor of your company, with the Gentlemen of your family, to dine with the Citizens of Alexandria, at Gadsby's tavern on thursday next at two oclock."[218]

As George Washington arrived at Gadsby's Tavern in Alexandria on March 22, 1797, he had served two terms as president since 1789. Washington's return brought him back into the social and economic life of Alexandria once again. A military escort brought him into Alexandria accompanied by fifteen cannon discharges. The party had sixteen formal toasts as part of a "splendid and plentiful dinner." Mayor Peyton delivered a "cordial and affectionate address." Washington reciprocated the warm remarks with a toast: "Prosperity to the Town and Citizens of Alexandria."[219] Alexandria welcomed George Washington back from his service in the Revolutionary War on December 31, 1783. Its citizens toasted his departure to serve as president of the United States on April 16, 1789. Yet again, the citizens of Alexandria welcomed His Excellency George Washington back home after serving his country as first president.

When Washington returned to Mount Vernon in 1797, there was a lot of work that needed to be done across his five farms. Washington was eager to get Mount Vernon back to economic vibrancy. After the deaths of Washington's nephew George Augustine Washington and another estate manager named Anthony Whitting, Mount Vernon was managed by William Pearce, who worked there from 1793 until 1796.[220] In October 1796,

George Washington's reconstructed distillery at Mount Vernon, which still operates today using eighteenth-century methods to produce whiskey. *Photo by the author.*

Washington contracted James Anderson, a native of Scotland, to work as his farm manager.[221] As a businessman, Washington was always innovative and willing to take calculated risks, such as the decision to switch from tobacco to wheat in the 1760s. As a result, when Anderson approached Washington with a unique idea that he believed would be profitable, Washington was intrigued by it. Anderson specifically pitched Washington the idea of a distillery. Anderson saw enormous potential to build a distillery along Dogue Run adjacent to Washington's gristmill.

While Washington liked the idea of a distillery, he had no expertise in distilling whiskey, nor did he know whether the whiskey would sell. He did know that his friend John Fitzgerald had a distillery in Alexandria.[222] So, Washington wrote to Fitzgerald and explained, "Mr Anderson *has* engaged me in a distillery, on a small scale, and is very desirous of encreasing it."[223] Washington added, "The thing is new to me, in toto; but in a distillery of another kind (Molasses) you must have a good general knowledge of its profits, & whether a ready sale of the Spirit[s] is to be calculated on from grain (principally to be raised on my own Farms) and the offal of my Mill. I, therefore, have taken the liberty of asking your opinion on the proposition of Mr Anderson."[224]

On June 12, 1797, Fitzgerald replied, "As I have no doubt but Mr Anderson understands the Distillation of Spirit from Grain I cannot hesitate in my Opinion that it might be carried on to great advantage on your Estate."[225] On the question of whether there existed a market for whiskey, Fitzgerald assured Washington, "[A]s to a Sale of the Whiskey there can be no doubt if the Quantity was ten times as much as he can make provided it is of a good Quality."[226]

On the advice of Fitzgerald, Washington decided to move forward with Anderson's proposal to build a distillery. The distillery was completed by the spring of 1798. In the last year of Washington's life, 1799, he recorded a "total sale of 10,942 gallons of whiskey, valued at $7,674."[227] In 2025, the value of sales would be approximately $200,000. Most importantly, Washington found his market for whiskey in Alexandria.

As Fitzgerald predicted, it sold well among his friends and neighbors in Alexandria. According to Mount Vernon's Digital Encyclopedia, George Washington's "best customer was his close friend George Gilpin," who sold Washington's whiskey at his store in Alexandria.[228] Furthermore, Gilpin was not the only merchant who bought and sold Washington's whiskey, as "other Alexandria merchants also bought large quantities to resell."[229] Thanks to Washington's friends in Alexandria like Fitzgerald and Gilpin, his distillery became one of the most profitable lines of business at Mount Vernon.

## A Flourishing Port City

During the 1790s, Washington, D.C., was being established as the permanent seat of America's capital. As a result, Alexandria saw a major boom in economic development. The population nearly doubled to slightly under five thousand by 1800. Washington's friends and leading citizens of Alexandria played a critical role in the continued development and economic vibrancy of the city.

One of the most noteworthy symbols of Alexandria's growing influence and wealth was the new City Hotel and Tavern, which was built in 1792. The tavern was an extension of a simpler, Georgian-style tavern constructed in 1785. The larger tavern was built on the corner of North Royal and Cameron Streets. It had many rooms, private dining spaces, and an elegant ballroom for entertainment. In 1796, John Gadsby leased the tavern from the owner, John Wise. Gadsby ran the tavern for the next twelve years. On Monday, February 12, 1798, George Washington wrote, "Went with the family to a Ball in Alexa. given by the Citizen[s] of it & its vicinity in commemoration of the Anniversary of my birth day."[230] Alexandria's citizens chose to celebrate Washington's birthday based on the Julian or Old-Style calendar. When Washington was born, the British were using this calendar but switched to the Gregorian calendar in 1752. The switch moved the date from February 11 to February 22. Washington's birthday celebration was on Monday, February 12, 1798, because February 11 was on a Sunday.[231]

*Top*: Gadsby's Tavern in Alexandria, which was opened in 1792 and leased to John Gadsby in 1796 by owner John Wise. The tavern hosted George Washington, Thomas Jefferson, and other leading figures of the era. *Photo by the author.*

*Bottom*: Captain's Row, a historic cobblestone street in Old Town Alexandria. Dating to the eighteenth century, it is one of the city's most historic and picturesque blocks. *Photo by the author.*

When Washington celebrated his birthday in Alexandria in 1798, the city was flourishing. Perhaps nothing highlights the growing prosperity of Alexandria more than the development of the shoreline and the cobblestones that were being laid on the streets. In fact, Washington's friend, fellow veteran, and business partner George Gilpin was Alexandria's commissioner for paving and grading streets. In this latter job, he was responsible for the development of Alexandria's streets after the shoreline was extended through a process of "banking out." Alexandria was originally founded on a high bluff overlooking a crescent-shaped bay that contained marshy mud flats called the "shoals." However, much of the bluff was cut down and filled in with dirt, soil, and debris. As the shoals were filled in, piers were built that extended into the deep water of the Potomac River for ships to dock. Additionally, roads were paved with stones that were oval shaped and exceeded sixty pounds.

After his presidency and in the same year as his sixty-sixth birthday at Gadsby's Tavern, George Washington noted the impressive development of Alexandria in a letter to his old friend Sally Fairfax, who was the wife of George William Fairfax. He marveled at the developments in Alexandria and its potential to be a world-class commercial city. Washington wrote, "Alexandria, within the last seven years, (since the establishment of the General Government) has increased in buildings, in population, in the improvement of its Streets by well executed pavements, and in the extension of its Wharves, in a manner, of which you can have very little idea."[232] Washington added that part of the prosperity owed to the "opening of the Inland navigation of Potomack River."[233] Finally, he concluded that "if this Country can stear clear of European Politics, stand firm on its bottom & be wise and temperate in its government, it bids fair to be one of the greatest & happiest nations in the world."[234] However, when Washington penned the letter to Sally Fairfax, it was not entirely clear that America would be able to stay clear of European politics. In fact, despite the growing prosperity of Alexandria in 1798, the drumbeats of war were once again beating loudly.

## The Quasi-War

As Britain and France went to war in 1792, both countries seized many American ships that they suspected of trading with the other country. In 1794, John Jay was sent to Britain as an American commissioner to negotiate a treaty. After successful negotiations, the U.S. Senate ratified the Jay Treaty with Great Britain in 1795. While America avoided conflict with Britain, the second-order effect was to antagonize France. In fact, during the period between October 1796 and July 1797, the French navy seized more than three hundred American commercial ships.[235]

President John Adams dealt with the accelerating tensions with France when he assumed office in March 1797. Initially, America responded by not paying its war debts to France. By October 1797, President Adams sent three commissioners—Charles Cotesworth Pinckney, John Marshall, and Elbridge Gerry—to France to negotiate an end to the hostilities and normalize relations. However, the American commissioners were initially refused a meeting with France's Foreign Minister Talleyrand. Instead, their French counterparts—who were given redacted codenames "X," "Y," and "Z"—bribed them, demanded loans, and sought an apology from America. This incident, known as the XYZ Affair, was a significant scandal, and the French treatment of the American delegation only enflamed the tensions. When two of the commissioners, Marshall and Pinckney, left France in April 1798, no agreement had been reached.

By May 1798, the prospects of war with France seemed high, and many Americans feared that France might invade the United States. As a result, President Adams declared May 9, 1798, a "day of Solemn Humiliation, Fasting, and Prayer." On that day, George Washington traveled to Alexandria and attended a service at the First Presbyterian Church in

*Left*: The Old Presbyterian Meeting House in Alexandria, founded in 1772. The congregation played a strong role in providing manpower during the American Revolution, and the church later hosted George Washington's memorial service in 1799. *Photo by the author.*

*Right*: Plaque at the Old Presbyterian Meeting House in Alexandria, noting George Washington's attendance on May 9, 1798, during a national day of humiliation, fasting, and prayer proclaimed by President John Adams during the Quasi-War with France. *Photo by the author.*

Alexandria, which is known today as the Old Presbyterian Meeting House. Reverend Dr. James Muir preached a sermon from the book of Genesis about Jacob's sons establishing the twelve tribes of Israel.[236] Reverend Muir hoped to inspire his fellow citizens with a powerful sermon and paid a compliment to Washington when he declared, "We have amongst us true patriots. Both the present and the late [i.e., previous] President know the true interests of their country."[237] Washington and his Alexandria friends prayed for peace during the service. Perhaps Washington suspected that war might require his country to call on him yet again. If he did think that was the case, he was proven right.

On July 4, 1798, President Adams commissioned George Washington "Lieutenant General and Commander in Chief of all the Armies raised or to be raised for the service of the United States."[238] General Washington held this commission until the day that he died on December 14, 1799, nearly seventeen months in total. President Adams took several steps to mobilize America's defenses and deter any potential French invasion. On April 30, 1798, the U.S. Department of the Navy was formally established under the War Department.[239] Simultaneously, an army was raised to prepare for the defenses of America.

As commander-in-chief, George Washington quickly began assembling a staff and making key appointments to help him manage the army.

Controversy ensued because Washington elevated his former aide-de-camp and treasury secretary, Alexander Hamilton, over his former general and secretary of war, Henry Knox. Henry Knox refused to serve under Hamilton. Washington's decision led to irreparable damage between his and Knox's friendship.

While Washington's decision with respect to one of his longtime friends, Knox, was controversial, there was one decision that engendered no controversy. Washington appointed his friend and doctor James Craik to the position of physician general in the U.S. Army. As hostilities escalated in the spring of 1798, Craik made multiple visits to Mount Vernon, including four visits on April 22, April 24, April 26–27, and April 30. Dr. Craik gladly accepted the appointment to be the Army's leading doctor. This selection was the culmination of years of service and deep trust between Washington and Craik. Since the Battle of Fort Necessity in 1754, Washington and Craik fought together in two wars. Among all the appointees, Craik served with Washington longer than anyone.[240]

## Alexandria Prepares for War...Again

In 1753, Washington left Alexandria for the Ohio Country at the beginning of what became the French and Indian War. Since that time, Washington and Alexandria experienced two major wars. During the French and Indian War, Washington raised and drilled troops in Alexandria. As the Revolutionary War approached, Washington commanded the Fairfax County Independent Company. From 1774 to 1775, he mustered and trained troops in Alexandria. In 1798, Washington and Alexandria prepared a third time for war. The local militia, known as the Alexandria Blues, formed a company to defend America from invasion by France.

On July 4, 1798, the same day Washington was commissioned as lieutenant general, Washington recorded that he "[w]ent up to the Celebration of the anniversary of Independance and dined in the Spring Gardens near Alexa. with a large Compa. of the Civil & Military of Fairfax County."[241] Washington was escorted into Alexandria "by a discharge of sixteen guns" and "a detachment from the troop of Dragoons."[242] Washington was in full uniform as he reviewed the troops that proceeded from Alexandria's King Street to Christ Church Episcopal.[243]

Additionally, a unit of men forty-five years and older was formed in Alexandria known as the Greyheads. Washington wrote to James McHenry that "the Greyheads of Alexandria, pretty numerous it seems, and composed of all the respectable old People of the place; having formed themselves into a company for the defence of the Town & its Vicinity, are in want of Colours; and it being intimated that the Presentation of them by Mrs Washington would be flattering to them; I take the liberty of requesting the favour of you to have made & sent to me as soon as is convenient, such as will be appropriate to the occasion."[244] Colonel Charles Simms was the commanding officer of the Greyheads. The Greyheads did accept colors that were delivered to them albeit incomplete. Washington had them "completed—at my expence—in Alexandria" in anticipation of a "grand parade."[245]

On October 30, the colors were used as part of President Adams's birthday celebration. According to the *Columbian Mirror* and *Alexandria Gazette*, "A stand of colours, presented by the respected consort of our venerable Cincinnatus to the Company of Silver Grays, was displayed for the first time on that day; and, although a variety of incidents prevented their being entirely completed, they had a very elegant appearance—The colours are composed of white silk; the device is, however, on an azure blue ground. The Golden Eagle of America has a portrait of General Washington suspended from its beak; in one talon a bunch of arrows, in the other a branch of Olive; and is surmounted by 16 stars, indicative of the number of States—The Motto—'Firm in Defence of Our Country.'"[246]

Despite the buoyant energy of troops mobilizing in Alexandria, the Quasi-War did not become a formal war. The Alexandria Blues and Greyheads did not have to fight off a French invasion at the foot of King Street. In fact, the extent of Washington's service was a five-week trip to Philadelphia to discuss the army's administration. On November 5, 1798, Washington began his journey to Philadelphia accompanied by a military escort in Alexandria under "Colonel Fitzgerald's and Captain Young's troops of cavalry, and the company of Alexandria blues."[247] As General Washington passed Gadsby's Tavern, the Alexandria Blues fired a sixteen-round salute.[248] Washington was then accompanied by his Alexandria military escorts to the "Ferry at George Town."[249]

The meetings in Philadelphia involved "selecting officers for twelve new regiments."[250] In reviewing the officer candidates from Virginia, Washington, Alexander Hamilton, and Charles Cotesworth Pinckney discussed six candidates. One of the candidates was Alexandrian Robert Young, who had been part of Washington's escort on November 5.

Fitzgerald and Simms both recommended Young, who was described as a "Young Gentleman desirous of serving his Country from zeal & activity can raise troops will do honor to his Country."[251] Furthermore, Robert T. Hooe also suggested Captain Young "of the Alexandria Troop" as well as Dr. Craik's son, George Washington Craik. Washington specifically mentioned to Secretary of War James McHenry that Craik "was in my family," which was a reference to the fact that Craik's son served as secretary to Washington during his presidency.[252]

While the army was never called into service, the Quasi-War period shows how George Washington and Alexandria made vigorous preparations as they had in two previous wars. Washington was back in uniform yet again. He continued to hold an active-duty commission until the day he died on December 14, 1799. One month before Washington's death, on November 9, 1799, Napoleon Bonaparte took control of France. In early 1800, France, under Napoleon, and America engaged in more productive diplomatic talks that ended hostilities and concluded America's two-year Quasi-War.

## The Final Year (1799)

Despite the looming threat of war, there were many peaceful moments and happy times that followed the November 1798 meeting in Philadelphia. Washington returned to Mount Vernon in December 1798. The year 1799 was the last year of George Washington's life, and he celebrated his sixty-seventh birthday party in Alexandria. Yet again, the celebration was based off the Julian calendar date. On February 11, 1799, Washington wrote, "Went up to Alexandria to the celebration of my birth day. Many Manœuvres were performed by the Uniform Corps and an elegant Ball & Supper at Night."[253] If Washington had lived to sixty-eight years old, he likely would have celebrated his birthday again at Gadsby's Tavern on February 11, 1800.

As the weather warmed, Washington entertained guests from Alexandria on a regular basis at Mount Vernon. He also traveled frequently to Alexandria. On April 3–4, 1799, George Washington lodged at the home of William Fitzhugh. The Federal-style home is located at 607 Oronoco Street and was built in 1795. Fitzhugh had a distinguished political career dating back to his service in the House of Burgesses (1772–74), Virginia Revolutionary

Conventions (1774–76), the Second Continental Congress (1779), and service as a member of the Virginia House of Delegates and Senate. Fitzhugh's property was later rented to Henry "Light-Horse Harry" Lee in 1811. By that time, Lee had several children, including a four-year-old son, Robert E. Lee, who spent many years of his childhood in the home until he left Alexandria to attend the U.S. Military Academy at West Point in 1825.

The Lee-Fendall House in Alexandria, built in 1785 for Philip Richard Fendall. The home is closely connected to the Lee family, including Henry "Light-Horse Harry" Lee, Revolutionary War cavalry officer and father of Robert E. Lee. *Photo by the author.*

Also in April 1799, Washington wrote that he went to Alexandria "to an Election of a Representative from the District to Congress & from the County to the State Legisla[tur]e."[254] In this election, Washington's friend Henry Lee won a seat in the House of Representatives for the Sixth Congress of the United States.[255]

Another important trip to Alexandria was on July 4, 1799, for an Independence Day celebration. Washington noted that he "dined with a number of the Citizens there in celebration of the anniversary of the declaration of American Independence at Kemps Tavern."[256] Kemps Tavern was formerly Wise's Tavern, where Washington had celebrated the Constitution's ratification and was toasted as the new president-elect on April 16, 1789.

Throughout 1799, Washington and the rest of the United States anticipated the new capital being permanently located on the shores of the Potomac River. Congress was scheduled to move in 1800 from Philadelphia to Washington, D.C. To encourage growth and development of the new capital city, George Washington bought lots on Capitol Hill. Furthermore, in late 1798, Washington made plans to build two adjoining townhouses on one of his Capitol Hill lots. However, he was worried that he might not have the cash to pay for the construction.

Washington had hoped to receive cash from the sale of some landholdings. But the sale was delayed, and he was getting nervous about having enough money. As a result, Washington turned to the Bank of Alexandria. On October 4, 1798, Washington wrote to Bank of Alexandria President William Herbert and explained, "Observing to you, not long since, that the want of money prevented my doing something (I have forgot now what) you said, if I understood you rightly, that I might be accommodated at the Bank of Alexandria."[257] On October 5, Herbert replied to Washington that he could receive loans in the form of sixty-day discount notes "from six to ten thousand dollars."[258] It is worth noting that Herbert was married to Sarah Carlyle Herbert, who was the last surviving child of John Carlyle, specifically from his first marriage to Sarah Fairfax Carlyle. In fact, Sarah Carlyle Herbert was named after her mother. Thus, we see the connection again of Washington with Alexandria and the second generation of Alexandrians.

Washington made his first payment of $500 from the Bank of Alexandria on December 20, 1798.[259] Washington made the checks payable to William Thornton, first architect of the Capitol, who had subcontracted the construction of George Washington's two adjoining Capitol Hill townhomes to George Blagden. The first payment was a cash payment.

However, by the summer of 1799, Washington still had not received money from the sale of his land. Thus, he was faced with the liquidity crunch he had worried might happen. Nevertheless, he had already engaged the Bank of Alexandria the previous fall. In June 1799, Washington used the bank's resources and secured a sixty-day discount note (i.e., short-term loan). At the end of August, Washington renewed the discount note for another sixty days. He sought another renewal in November. Without the Bank of Alexandria, George Washington would not have been able to build his townhouses on Capitol Hill.

On November 6, 1799, Washington had a chance to "view my building [in] the Federal City."[260] It was nearly completed. Washington's cost was approximately $12,000. His goal was to sell the property for $15,000. In a letter dated October 6, Washington wrote to Thornton to let him know if he "should hear of any person, or persons, disposed to buy."[261] One of the last checks that George Washington wrote in his life was to William Thornton. The check was issued from the Bank of Alexandria. It was written on November 26, 1799, in the amount of $906.57.[262] The payment was to put the finishing touches on the exterior of the home. Specifically, Washington had the townhouses rusticated in the same style as the Mansion House at Mount Vernon. This means that the wood was painted and sand was applied to the painted wood to give the house the look of stone.

George Washington never lived to see the completed townhomes or see them sold. According to Washington's will, the value he placed on his lots was $15,000. The executors of his estate rented the property. Washington's townhomes were "unexpectedly consumed by fire" during the War of 1812.[263] The homes were later remodeled and used as a boardinghouse and hotel. In the early twentieth century, the government had the buildings razed, and a plaque has been placed at the original spot of Washington's townhomes.[264]

In the last months of his life, George Washington had a lot on his mind besides the construction of his townhouses on Capitol Hill. Not only was he leaning on Alexandria for financial assistance, but he was also seeking spiritual comfort within the walls of Christ Church. On November 17, Washington recorded, "Went to Church in Alexandria & dined with Mr. Fitzhugh."[265] Washington had owned his pew in Christ Church for twenty-six years since purchasing it in February 1773. Washington had attended services during critical moments in America's history. On November 17, perhaps he had a lot on his mind personally. Two months prior, his younger brother Charles Washington passed away. Washington had outlived his nine siblings, which included four from his father's first marriage and five from the second marriage to Washington's mother. Washington didn't know that November 17, 1799, would be the last time he attended a church service in his life. He attended that last service in Alexandria at Christ Church. One month later, Washington would follow his brother and siblings in death.

# Chapter 34

# WASHINGTON'S FINAL MOMENTS, DECEMBER 14, 1799

On December 12, 1799, George Washington "rode out to his farms" to inspect the work at Mount Vernon. It was a typical day but with "very bad, rain, hail and snow." Washington sat down to dinner while still wearing his clothes from riding in the weather. Tobias Lear wrote a detailed account of the events that led to Washington's death and noted that Washington's "neck appeared to be wet and the snow was hanging upon his hair."

On December 13, Washington felt a cold accompanied with a "sore throat" and "hoarseness." Washington refused to take medicine for his cold. Between 2:00 a.m. and 3:00 a.m. on Saturday, December 14, Washington awoke Martha and felt a sharp pain in his throat. He struggled to breathe and could hardly speak. Lear arrived in Washington's bed chamber and observed Washington "breathing with difficulty." He sent for Washington's farm overseer, George Rawlins, to bleed him. Lear also dispatched a messenger to Alexandria to get Washington's friend and personal physician Dr. James Craik.

Early in the morning, Dr. Craik heard a knock on his door at 210 Duke Street in Alexandria. He immediately rode ten miles from Alexandria to Mount Vernon and arrived sometime shortly after 9:00 a.m. Rawlins had already bled Washington a half pint of blood over the objections of Martha but at the insistence of George. Lear described that "[Craik] put a blister of Cantharides on the Throat, took some more blood from him, and had a gargle of Vinegar, & sage tea, and ordered some Vinegar & hot water for him to inhale the steam, which he did; but in attempting to use the gargle he was almost suffocated."

When Craik observed the severity of Washington's condition, he requested help from another Alexandria doctor, Dr. Elisha Cullen Dick. Dr. Brown from Port Tobacco, Maryland, had also been sent to help. But Craik feared that Brown might arrive too late. After sending for Dr. Dick, Craik bled Washington again. Bloodletting was a common practice in the eighteenth century based on medical theories that illnesses were caused by an imbalance of "humors" or bodily fluids. Bleeding was believed to rebalance the fluids. This medical practice is now outdated and thankfully no longer used. Unfortunately, it is estimated that George Washington may have lost five pints of blood or roughly half his total blood supply.[266]

George Washington more than likely had an inflammation of his epiglottis and a condition known as epiglottitis. Modern medicine such as antibiotics could remedy this condition quickly. Unfortunately, no such medicine existed in 1799. Lear said that Dr. Dick arrived around three o'clock, and "[u]pon Dr Dick's seeing the General, and consulting a few minutes with Dr Craik, he was bled again." Dr. Brown arrived. The doctors held a conference to decide what to do next. Dr. Dick was a younger doctor. Washington knew him not only through his medical practice but also since he was the worshipful master of the Alexandria Freemason Lodge No. 22 of which Washington was also a member. Readers will recall Dr. Dick was present at the laying of the cornerstone of both the capital city of Washington, D.C., in 1791 and the U.S. Capitol in 1793.

The three doctors held a conference, and Dr. Dick proposed the idea of a tracheotomy. However, the doctors did not do it. Perhaps they were concerned that Washington had lost too much blood and fluids. They may have determined that it was too risky. They had little options left. As the afternoon turned into early evening, George Washington graciously thanked his doctors. He turned to Dr. Craik and said, "Doctor, I die hard; but I am not afraid to go, I believed from my first attack, that I should not survive it; my breath cannot last long."

From Lear's detailed account of Washington's last day, one powerful moment was when Washington sent for a copy of two wills. He made the decision to keep one will and discard another. It is widely accepted that the will he kept was rewritten specifically to direct the manumission of George Washington's 123 enslaved individuals at Mount Vernon. Lear also explained that Washington noticed that Christopher Sheels, an enslaved servant, had been standing in the bedchamber for a long time and "made a motion for him to sit."[267] The significance of this act underscores Washington's compassion and thoughtfulness even at the end of his life. His Excellency General Washington was in tremendous pain yet still considerate of other people.

Lear noted that Dr. Craik was "overcome with grief." Craik and Washington served together for forty-five years. Craik had taken care of Washington through numerous illnesses. Perhaps Craik recalled being with George Washington in 1755 during the Braddock Campaign. Washington had dysentery and struggled for days in the back of a wagon. George Washington was now sixty-seven and endured one of the most violent sicknesses of his life. As he realized that there was nothing left for him to do, Craik must have felt helpless and knew that the end was near.

Finally, Washington tried to speak and said, "Have me decently buried; and do not let my body be put in the vault in less than three days after I am dead." Lear did not respond initially. Washington prompted him to acknowledge the request, saying, "Do you understand me?" Lear replied, "Yes." Washington uttered his last words: "'Tis well." Ten more minutes passed. Dr. Craik came to Washington's bedside as Lear took Washington's hand and "put it into my bosom." At which point, "Dr Craik put his hands over his Eyes *and he expired without a struggle or a sigh!*"

Grave of Dr. James Craik at the Old Presbyterian Meeting House in Alexandria. Craik was George Washington's "compatriot in arms and old and intimate friend." *Photo by the author.*

On December 14, 1799, George Washington died at age sixty-seven years old. Martha came into the room and asked, "Is he gone?" Lear signaled that he was. Martha replied, "*Tis well….All is now over, I shall soon follow him! I have no more trials to pass through!*" For the next two years until her death in 1802, Martha no longer slept in the bedchamber that she had shared with George. Instead, she slept in the third-floor garret bedchamber that John Patterson had built in 1758. Dr. Craik continued to care for Martha up until the day of her death on May 22, 1802.

Dr. Craik did everything he could think of to save his friend. Furthermore, Dr. Dick is reported to have stopped a clock in the bedroom at 10:20 p.m., which is believed to be the time of Washington's death. It had been fifty years since Alexandria was founded in 1749 when Washington was seventeen years old. The city that young George had studied as a surveyor played an integral role in his development as a military officer, his success as a businessman, and his career as a politician. The relationship had been solidified in war and peace. Washington had leaned heavily on Alexandria up to the moment that he took his last breath.

## Chapter 35

# HONORING GEORGE WASHINGTON

News of Washington's death spread quickly on December 15. His Excellency General Washington, father of America, leading citizen of Alexandria, had passed away at Mount Vernon. It is hard to comprehend the magnitude of this moment and how much sorrow people felt. George Washington held a distinguished and esteemed position in the hearts and minds of his countrymen. He was a man above reproach. While he was human and prone to the vices that afflict all human beings, he was a man of exemplary character. He was a servant who put country above self since his first mission to the Ohio Country in 1753.

Washington's request to be buried at least three days after his death was due to a common fear that he might still be alive. Washington did not want a big funeral and preferred to be "interred in a private manner." Nevertheless, funeral preparations quickly took place in Alexandria. Tobias Lear ordered a mahogany coffin "to be made for a body 6 feet 3½ inches long, 1 foot 9 inches 'Across the Shoulders,' and 2 feet 'Across the Elbows.'"[268] As part of funeral preparations, Lear had the family vault opened on Monday, December 16, and cleared of "rubbish."

The date of Washington's funeral was set for Wednesday, December 18, 1799, at Mount Vernon. This was hardly enough time for news to reach people in other states and allow for them to travel to Mount Vernon. However, it provided plenty of time for Alexandrians to make the trip. In fact, making the trip to Mount Vernon from Alexandria included the local militia known as the Alexandria Blues, which had rallied to Washington's support during the Quasi-War in 1798. Alexandria's Freemasons from Lodge No. 22 also arrived to take place in the funeral procession and performed a series of funeral rites for their brother Mason. As a result, Lear ordered food and drinks from Alexandria.

George Washington's funeral was both a military funeral and a Masonic service. There were several people who spoke at Washington's funeral from Alexandria. Reverend Thomas Davis from Christ Church read from the Episcopal Book of Common Prayer. Reverend James Muir, who was pastor of the Presbyterian Church and chaplain of Alexandria's Masonic Lodge No. 22, officiated. He was joined by worshipful master of Alexandria Lodge No. 22 Dr. Elisha Cullen Dick, who also delivered words as part of the Masonic rites. Another Presbyterian minister, Reverend William Maffatt, also spoke. Maffatt was also a Freemason and a teacher at the Alexandria Academy.

The cavalry from Alexandria escorted the bier and the procession to the family vault. There were six honorary pallbearers who flanked the bier with three men on both sides. Five of these men were fellow Masons and close friends of George Washington. These included George Gilpin, Charles Simms, Charles Little, Dennis Ramsay, and William Payne. The sixth honorary pallbearer, who was not a Mason, was Philip Marsteller. The honorary pallbearers were all ranked as colonels in the local militia. The bier bearers were all lieutenants in the 106$^{th}$ Virginia Regiment. They were Lieutenants Lawrence Hooff Jr., James Turner, George Wise, and William Moss.

However, there was a fifth bier bearer, who stepped in when one of the bier bearers, Lieutenant William Moss, apparently became ill, injured, or was simply unable to carry the casket. This is the story about a man named George Coryell. Coryell was originally from New Jersey, and his family ran a ferry known as Coryell's Ferry, which played a pivotal role in helping Washington's army traverse the frigid waters of the Delaware River notably on the evening of December 25–26, 1776, to attack the Hessian garrison at Trenton, New Jersey. During the Battle of Trenton, Lieutenant James Monroe (later America's fifth president) was shot in the shoulder and recovered from his wounds at the Coryell home.

In the 1790s, as Alexandria was going through a major economic boom, George Coryell moved to Alexandria and worked as a carpenter. He lived at 206 Duke Street and was a neighbor of Dr. James Craik. He was one of many Alexandrians present at George Washington's funeral on December 18. When William Moss could not carry the bier, Coryell stepped in and carried it. This does not appear to have been planned, but it means that there were five bier bearers who helped carry George

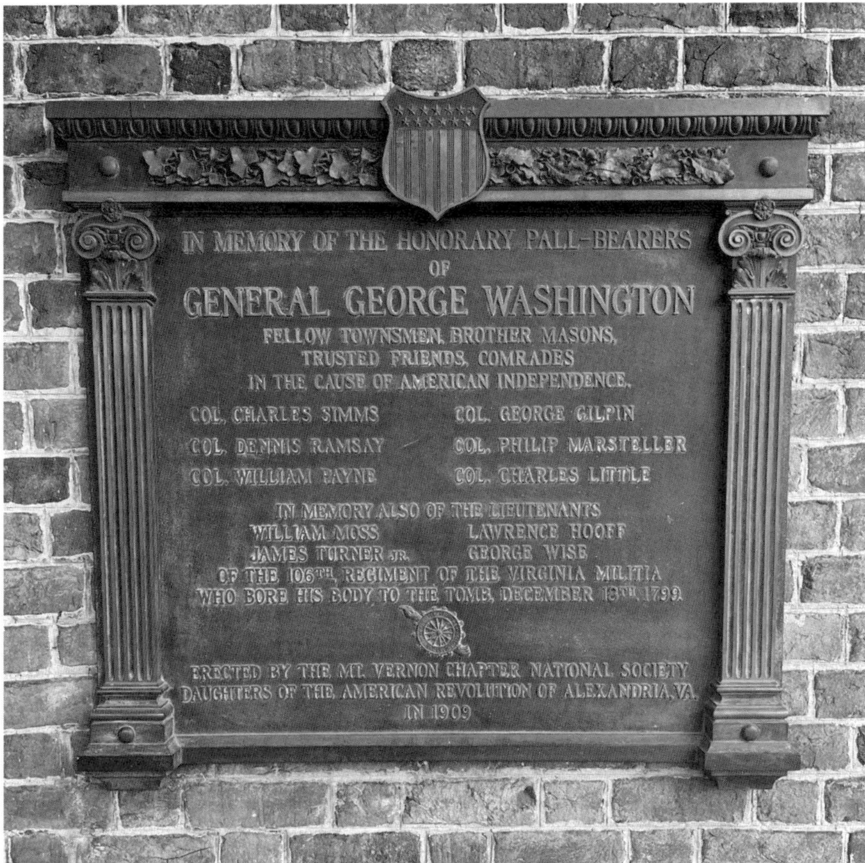


Plaque honoring the pallbearers of George Washington, many of whom were members of Christ Church in Alexandria. *Photo by the author.*

Washington to the family vault at his funeral. It is worth noting that George Coryell was one of the oldest surviving pallbearers, having lived to February 18, 1850.[269] He is currently interred at a Presbyterian burial ground in Lambertville, New Jersey.

Since Washington's funeral was not widely attended beyond Alexandria, one of the only public officials who joined in Washington's funeral procession was the mayor of Alexandria Francis Peyton. It was the same Mayor Peyton who toasted Washington at Gadsby's Tavern on March 22, 1797. It is fitting that most of the people at Washington's funeral were from Alexandria. It was the city that was founded by his older brother Lawrence and his benefactor, Colonel William Fairfax. It was the city that honored Washington at his homecoming from the Revolutionary War in 1783 and his presidency in

1797. Dennis Ramsay, who first hailed Washington as president on April 16, 1789, was now marching alongside his casket. Washington had done the same for his father, William Ramsay, in 1785.

When the news of Washington's death spread, businesses shut down throughout the United States. Cities and towns in America went into a period of mourning and held their own memorial services. Four memorial services were held in Alexandria at the Presbyterian church. Two weeks after Washington's funeral at Mount Vernon, there was a Congressional memorial service in Philadelphia that took place at the German Lutheran Church. During this service, George Washington's longtime friend and Revolutionary War cavalry officer Henry "Light-Horse Harry" Lee delivered the Congressional eulogy with the most famous quote attributed to George Washington that he was "first in war, first in peace, first in the hearts of his countrymen." It was a fitting tribute from Henry Lee, who had served under Washington during the Revolutionary War and the Whiskey Rebellion and was a political ally in the fight to ratify the Constitution.

Washington was certainly first in the hearts of his friends and neighbors in Alexandria. He reciprocated the love and respect of many of them. In his will, Washington left items to his friends. He described Dr. James Craik as "my compatriot in arms, and old & intimate friend" and gave him "my Bureau (or as the Cabinet makers call it, Tambour Secretary) and the circular chair—an appendage of my Study."[270] Washington left his friend Dr. David Stuart "my large shaving & dressing Table, and my Telescope." His friend Bryan Fairfax, who was another son of Colonel William Fairfax, was given "a Bible in three large folio volumes, with notes." Tobias Lear was left the "farm that he now holds." Washington also left $4,000 or twenty shares of stock in the Bank of Alexandria to the Alexandria Academy.

Finally, there was only one property that Washington left outright to his wife, Martha. It was the half-acre lot on the corner of North Pitt and Cameron Streets, which he purchased in 1763. He built his townhouse on the lot from 1769 to 1771. After Washington bought the lot in 1763, Alexandria expanded and grew in prominence. Washington grew with it. Their fates were inextricably linked. The first item that Washington wrote about in his will was the Alexandria townhome. He wrote, "To my dearl[y be]loved wife Martha Washington [I] give and bequeath the use, profit [an]d benefit of my whole Estate, real and p[er]sonal, for the term of her natural li[fe]—except such parts thereof as are sp[e]cifically disposed of hereafter: [My i]mproved lot in the Town of Alex[andria, situated on] Pitt & Cameron [Streets, I give to her and] her heirs forev[er]."[271]

# EPILOGUE

On December 2, 1853, a woman identified as a "Southern Matron" wrote a letter that was published in the *Charleston Mercury*.[272] In the letter, the Southern Matron called on ladies of the South to rally to the cause of saving George Washington's home, Mount Vernon. The writer was Ann Pamela Cunningham, who was a great-granddaughter of Alexandria's John Dalton. Dalton served with George Washington during the French and Indian War and conducted extensive business with Washington through the firm Carlyle & Dalton.

Cunningham's letter was inspired by what her mother witnessed to be the terrible state of disrepair and dilapidation of Mount Vernon. While Cunningham called on southern ladies, her letter resonated nationally. Over the next five years, she worked tirelessly to raise $200,000 to purchase Washington's Mount Vernon. Her organization was named the Mount Vernon Ladies' Association (MVLA). The MVLA raised the money in 1858 and completed the purchase in 1860. The last private owner of Mount Vernon was George Washington's great-grandnephew, John Augustine Washington III.[273]

The MVLA still owns and manages Mount Vernon to this day. It continues to restore and maintain the property. While Washington's landholdings around Mount Vernon were eight thousand acres at its peak, the property is now approximately five hundred acres. Every day, visitors come to Mount Vernon from all over the world. There are tours and programs continually taking place. There are special events and patriotic celebrations that are all

*Left*: Portrait of Ann Pamela Cunningham, founder of the Mount Vernon Ladies' Association, who led the effort to preserve George Washington's estate in 1853. *Courtesy of Mount Vernon.*

*Opposite*: Statue of George Washington at the George Washington Masonic National Memorial in Alexandria, which honors Washington's role as a Freemason and national leader. *Photo by the author.*

dedicated to remembering America's most revered founding father. Martha is also remembered along with other family members who lived at Mount Vernon. Furthermore, the stories of Washington and Martha's enslaved laborers are told and interpreted.

Since its creation in 1853, the MVLA has been the single most important organization involved in the education, remembrance, and honoring of George Washington. The fact that Ann Pamela Cunningham was a descendant of one of Alexandria's trustees and town founders is no coincidence. Her great-grandfather would be proud to know of his posterity's commitment to his friend's legacy.

Today in Alexandria, George Washington's birthday party is still celebrated every February at Gadsby's Tavern. The city holds a parade annually on Monday during President's Day weekend. It is one of the most significant rituals that ensures Alexandria continues to play the leading role in honoring its most prominent citizen.

Alexandria's Freemason Lodge No. 22 also built a substantial nine-story stone memorial on a hilltop at the top of King Street on the outskirts

of today's portion of Alexandria known as "Old Town." The George Washington Masonic National Memorial is open for visitors and also houses an active Freemason Lodge called the Alexandria-Washington Lodge No. 22. The memorial is a shrine to its most beloved brother Mason.

Over the years, the City of Alexandria has explicitly claimed George Washington as its own. Marketing materials from past city brochures and advertisements have made the claim that Alexandria was George Washington's "hometown." Based solely on geographic proximity, this claim is substantiated. Alexandria remains the closest city to Mount Vernon. Guests and visitors frequently tour the two in conjunction with each other.

The Mount Vernon Memorial Parkway was built specifically for George Washington's bicentennial in 1932. The parkway runs through Alexandria along Washington Street. It is now known as the George Washington Memorial Parkway. The parkway was meant to take people along a scenic drive from Washington, D.C., to Mount Vernon. The City of Alexandria created a historic district in 1946. The goal was to regulate the look and architectural style of the buildings on Washington Street. In doing so, the city gave its Board of Architectural Review (BAR) authority to approve or deny exterior development of properties not only on Washington Street but also throughout the Old and Historic District, which became the third-oldest historic district in the United States.

Throughout Alexandria, there are dozens of historic markers, plaques, and monuments to George Washington. Each place that claims a critical piece of Washington history tells a different and unique story that allows visitors and locals to understand significant moments of George Washington's life. As a result, there is no city that can provide a more robust education about the entire scope of Washington's life than Alexandria.

Furthermore, there are dozens of historic people with extensive connections to Alexandria that were involved in every phase of Washington's life. These people were more than mere acquaintances. In the case of Washington's brothers, they were literally family. Some of them became extended family through marriage. The Fairfaxes were like family to Washington. Most of them, like Dr. James Craik, could be called "intimate friend[s]." As Henry Lee said of George Washington, he was "first in war and first in peace." His Alexandria friends were with him when he first went to war and when he returned to peace. Through their efforts of friendship, they helped ensure and solidify George Washington's reputation as "first in the hearts of his countrymen."

# NOTES

## *Preface*

1. George Washington to William Ramsay, January 29, 1769, National Archives, Founders Online, https://founders.archives.gov/documents/Washington/02-08-02-0126. Original source: *The Papers of George Washington, Colonial Series*, vol. 8, June 24, 1767–25, December 1771, ed. W.W. Abbot and Dorothy Twohig (University Press of Virginia, 1993), 167–68.
2. Freeman, *George Washington*, 3:211.

## *Chapter 1*

3. Freeman, *George Washington*, 1:194.
4. Mount Vernon Ladies' Association, George Washington's Mount Vernon Digital Encyclopedia, "Lawrence Washington."
5. Chernow, *Washington*, 16.
6. Chernow, *Washington*, 19–20.
7. Northern Virginia Regional Parks Authority, "Ties That Bind."
8. "George Washington's Professional Surveys," National Archives, Founders Online.
9. Berlau, *George Washington, Entrepreneur*.
10. Berlau, *George Washington, Entrepreneur*.

## *Chapter 2*

11. "Commission from Robert Dinwiddie, 30 October 1753," National Archives, Founders Online.
12. "Journey to the French Commandant: Narrative," National Archives, Founders Online.
13. "Journey to the French Commandant: Narrative," National Archives, Founders Online.

## *Chapter 3*

14. Carlyle, *Personal and Family Correspondence*.
15. Carlyle, *Personal and Family Correspondence.*
16. Carlyle, *Personal and Family Correspondence.*
17. Carlyle, *Personal and Family Correspondence.*
18. Carlyle, *Personal and Family Correspondence.*
19. Carlyle, *Personal and Family Correspondence.*
20. "Expedition to the Ohio, 1754: Narrative," National Archives, Founders Online.

## *Chapter 4*

21. Carlyle, *Personal and Family Correspondence.*
22. Carlyle, *Personal and Family Correspondence.*
23. Carlyle, *Personal and Family Correspondence.*
24. From George Washington to William Fairfax, April 23, 1755, National Archives, Founders Online.
25. Freeman, *George Washington*, 2:26.
26. Freeman, *George Washington*, 2:26.
27. Lefkowitz, *George Washington's Indispensable Men*, 91.

## *Chapter 5*

28. Anderson, *Crucible of War*, 108.
29. City of Alexandria, Virginia, "Historic Waterfront Chapter 1."

30. Freeman, *George Washington*, 2:2.
31. To George Washington from John Kirkpatrick, September 22, 1756, National Archives, Founders Online.
32. To George Washington from William Ramsay, September 22, 1756, National Archives, Founders Online.
33. To George Washington from William Ramsay, July 30, 1757, National Archives, Founders Online.
34. To George Washington from William Ramsay, July 30, 1757, National Archives, Founders Online.
35. To George Washington from William Ramsay, September 3, 1757, National Archives, Founders Online.
36. From George Washington to Robert Dinwiddie, October 24, 1757, National Archives, Founders Online.
37. To George Washington from Robert Dinwiddie, October 24, 1757, National Archives, Founders Online.

## *Chapter 6*

38. Fairfax County, Virginia, Deed Book D:693.
39. Freeman, *George Washington*, 2:266.
40. Freeman, *George Washington*, 2:266.
41. From George Washington to John Augustine Washington, May 28, 1755, National Archives, Founders Online.
42. Freeman, *George Washington*, 2:276.

## *Chapter 7*

43. From George Washington to John Blair, April 2, 1758, National Archives, Founders Online.
44. To George Washington from John Patterson, June 17, 1758, National Archives, Founders Online.
45. To George Washington from George William Fairfax, September 15, 1758, National Archives, Founders Online.

## *Chapter 8*

46. History Committee of the Alexandria Bicentennial, *Notes Prepared by the History Committee.*
47. Preisser, "Eighteenth-Century Alexandria, Virginia."
48. History Committee of the Alexandria Bicentennial, *Notes Prepared by the History Committee.*
49. "Memorandum Respecting the Militia, 1–2 May 1756," National Archives, Founders Online.
50. Washington, *Diaries*, April 17, 1760, National Archives, Founders Online.
51. Washington, *Diaries*, April 17, 1760, National Archives, Founders Online.
52. City of Alexandria, Virginia, "Waterfront History."
53. Chernow, *Washington*, 141.

## *Chapter 9*

54. City of Alexandria, Virginia, "History of Alexandria."
55. George Washington to Carlyle & Adam, February 15, 1767, National Archives, Founders Online.
56. Washington, *Diaries*, September 1769, National Archives, Founders Online.
57. Washington, *Diaries*, September 28, 1769, National Archives, Founders Online.
58. "Enclosure: Schedule of Property, 9 July 1799," National Archives, Founders Online.
59. Washington, *Diaries*, August 20, 1771, National Archives, Founders Online.
60. City of Alexandria, Virginia, "Alexandria History Museum."
61. Washington to Bushrod Washington, November 25, 1788, National Archives, Founders Online.
62. Washington to Fitzgerald, Herbert, and Gilpin, November 22, 1797, National Archives, Founders Online.

## *Chapter 10*

63. "Fairfax County Poll Sheet, 16 July 1765," National Archives, Founders Online.

## *Chapter 11*

64. From George Washington to John Dalton, February 15, 1773, National Archives, Founders Online.
65. From George Washington to John Dalton, February 15, 1773, National Archives, Founders Online.
66. Freeman, *George Washington*, 2:196.

## *Chapter 12*

67. Chernow, *Washington*, 153.
68. Washington, *Diaries*, January 3, 1768, National Archives, Founders Online.
69. Washington, *Diaries*, February 24, 1768, National Archives, Founders Online.
70. Washington, *Diaries*, June 6, 1768, National Archives, Founders Online.
71. Washington, *Diaries*, January 2, 1771, National Archives, Founders Online.
72. Chernow, *Washington*, 154.

## *Chapter 13*

73. Washington, *Diaries*, February 19, 1768, National Archives, Founders Online.
74. Washington to George Johnston, January 5, 1758, National Archives, Founders Online.
75. Washington, *Diaries*, January 1760, National Archives, Founders Online.
76. Washington from George Johnston, January 8, 1760, National Archives, Founders Online.
77. Washington to Robert Hanson Harrison, October 7, 1769, National Archives, Founders Online.
78. Washington, *Diaries*, December 1770, National Archives, Founders Online.
79. To George Washington from Robert Hanson Harrison, January 10, 1772, National Archives, Founders Online.

## *Chapter 14*

80. Washington, *Diaries*, July 1774, National Archives, Founders Online.
81. Washington, *Diaries*, July 1774, National Archives, Founders Online.
82. Washington, *Diaries*, July 1774, National Archives, Founders Online.

## *Chapter 15*

83. White, "Independent Companies of Virginia, 1774–1775," 149–62.
84. Fairfax Independent Company to George Washington, October 19, 1774, National Archives, Founders Online.
85. Fairfax Independent Company to George Washington, October 19, 1774, National Archives, Founders Online.
86. Fairfax Independent Company to George Washington, October 19, 1774, National Archives, Founders Online.
87. Fairfax Independent Company to George Washington, October 19, 1774, National Archives, Founders Online.
88. Washington, *Diaries*, November 13, 1774, National Archives, Founders Online.
89. *Historic Christ Church*.
90. Terrell, "Fairfax Militia During the Revolutionary War Period."
91. Washington, *Diaries*, January 16, 1775, National Archives, Founders Online.
92. Washington, *Diaries*, April 1775, National Archives, Founders Online.
93. Washington, *Diaries*, May 4, 1775, National Archives, Founders Online.
94. Fairfax Independent Company to George Washington, October 19, 1774, National Archives, Founders Online.

## *Chapter 16*

95. American Battlefield Trust, "Boston Battle Facts and Summary."
96. Ellis, *His Excellency*, 92.
97. Chernow, *Washington*, 235.
98. Chernow, *Washington*, 235.
99. Chernow, *Washington*, 236.
100. American Battlefield Trust, "Brooklyn."
101. McCullough, *1776*, 188.
102. McCullough, *1776*, 188.
103. Mount Vernon Ladies' Association, George Washington's Mount Vernon Digital Encyclopedia, "Battle of Kip's Bay."
104. Washington to Hancock, October 5, 1776, National Archives, Founders Online.
105. Mount Vernon Ladies' Association, George Washington's Mount Vernon Digital Encyclopedia, "New York Campaign."
106. Pennsylvania Historical & Museum Commission and WITF, "Excerpts from the diary of Colonel John Fitzgerald."

107. Pennsylvania Historical & Museum Commission and WITF, "Excerpts from the diary of Colonel John Fitzgerald."
108. American Battlefield Trust, "Trenton Battle Facts and Summary."
109. Ellis, *His Excellency*, 99.
110. Ellis, *His Excellency*, 99.

## *Chapter 17*

111. From George Washington to James Craik, April 26, 1777, National Archives, Founders Online.
112. To George Washington from James Craik, May 13, 1777, National Archives, Founders Online.
113. From George Washington to William Shippen Jr., February 6, 1777, National Archives, Founders Online.
114. Hand, "British Capture Philadelphia."

## *Chapter 18*

115. American Battlefield Trust, "When Did the American Revolution Begin?"
116. National Park Service, "Health and Medicine."
117. Ecelbarger, "Permanent Losses and New Gains."
118. Ecelbarger, "Permanent Losses and New Gains."
119. Ecelbarger, "Permanent Losses and New Gains."
120. Sinks, "Life and Times of Physician-General William Brown."

## *Chapter 19*

121. Mount Vernon Ladies' Association, George Washington's Mount Vernon Digital Encyclopedia, "Conway Cabal."
122. James Craik to George Washington, January 6, 1778, National Archives, Founders Online.
123. George Washington to Lieutenant Colonel John Fitzgerald, February 28, 1778, National Archives, Founders Online.
124. From George Washington to Lieutenant Colonel John Fitzgerald, February 28, 1778, National Archives, Founders Online.

125. Lieutenant Colonel John Fitzgerald to George Washington, March 17, 1778, National Archives, Founders Online.
126. Lieutenant Colonel John Fitzgerald to George Washington, March 17, 1778, National Archives, Founders Online.

## *Chapter 20*

127. "General Orders, 20 January 1778," National Archives, Founders Online.
128. George Washington to Captain Henry Lee Jr., January 20, 1778, National Archives, Founders Online.

## *Chapter 21*

129. Lefkowitz, *George Washington's Indispensable Men*, 169.
130. Lefkowitz, *George Washington's Indispensable Men*, 169.
131. Ellis, *His Excellency*, 120.
132. Lefkowitz, *George Washington's Indispensable Men*, 175.
133. National Park Service, "Lt Col John Fitzgerald."

## *Chapter 22*

134. O'Keefe, "American Revolution in Alexandria, Virginia."
135. American Battlefield Trust, "Charleston Battle Facts and Summary."
136. Northern Virginia Regional Parks Authority, "First Nine Months of 1780."
137. From Thomas Jefferson to John Fitzgerald, June 9, 1780, National Archives, Founders Online.
138. Wagener to Jefferson, April 3, 1781, National Archives, Founders Online.
139. Mount Vernon Ladies' Association, George Washington's Mount Vernon Digital Encyclopedia, "John Fitzgerald."
140. Rowland, Life of George Mason, 1:10.

## *Chapter 23*

141. From George Washington to James Hendricks, September 15, 1781, National Archives, Founders Online.

142. To George Washington from James Hendricks, September 20, 1781, National Archives, Founders Online.
143. To George Washington from James Hendricks, September 20, 1781, National Archives, Founders Online.
144. Mount Vernon Ladies' Association, George Washington's Mount Vernon Digital Encyclopedia, "John Parke Custis."
145. Mount Vernon Ladies' Association, George Washington's Mount Vernon Digital Encyclopedia, "Newburgh Conspiracy."
146. National Constitution Center, "Newburgh Address (1783)."

## *Chapter 24*

147. Ellis, *His Excellency*, 146.

## *Chapter 25*

148. From George Washington to William Brown, November 24, 1785, National Archives, Founders Online.
149. From George Washington to Trustees of the Alexandria Academy, December 17, 1785, National Archives, Founders Online.
150. "George Washington's Last Will and Testament, 9 July 1799," National Archives, Founders Online.
151. George Washington Masonic National Memorial Association, "Brief History."
152. National Park Service, "George Washington Inaugural Bible."
153. To George Washington from David Griffith, November 3, 1788, National Archives, Founders Online.
154. *Brick Chapel to Basilica.*
155. *Brick Chapel to Basilica.*
156. *Brick Chapel to Basilica.*

## *Chapter 26*

157. From George Washington to James Craik, July 10, 1784, National Archives, Founders Online.
158. Washington, *Diaries*, May 17, 1785, National Archives, Founders Online.

159. Washington, *Diaries*, May 17, 1785, National Archives, Founders Online.
160. Washington, *Diaries*, January 3, 1787, National Archives, Founders Online.
161. Washington, *Diaries*, January 17, 1785, National Archives, Founders Online.

## *Chapter 27*

162. "March 1785," National Archives, Founders Online.
163. Clan Henderson Society of the United States, "History's Hendersons."
164. To George Washington from Thomas Stone, January 28, 1785, National Archives, Founders Online.
165. Mount Vernon Ladies' Association, George Washington's Mount Vernon Digital Encyclopedia, "Mount Vernon Conference."

## *Chapter 28*

166. Henry Lee Jr. to George Washington, September 8, 1786, National Archives, Founders Online.
167. Mount Vernon Ladies' Association, George Washington's Mount Vernon Digital Encyclopedia, "Annapolis Convention."
168. Washington, *Diaries*, May 1787, National Archives, Founders Online.
169. Washington, *Diaries*, May 1787, National Archives, Founders Online.

## *Chapter 29*

170. To George Washington from David Stuart, November 8, 1786, National Archives, Founders Online.
171. To George Washington from David Stuart, November 8, 1786, National Archives, Founders Online.
172. George Washington to Charles Simms, September 22, 1786, National Archives, Founders Online.
173. George Washington to David Stuart, June 23, 1788, National Archives, Founders Online.
174. George Washington to David Stuart, June 8, 1788, National Archives, Founders Online.
175. Chernow, *Washington*, 546.

176. Washington, *Diaries*, June 1788, National Archives, Founders Online.
177. From George Washington to Charles Cotesworth Pinckney, June 28, 1788, National Archives, Founders Online.

## *Chapter 30*

178. George Washington to the Mayor, Corporation, and Citizens of Alexandria, April 16, 1789, National Archives, Founders Online.
179. George Washington to the Mayor, Corporation, and Citizens of Alexandria, April 16, 1789, National Archives, Founders Online.
180. George Washington to the Mayor, Corporation, and Citizens of Alexandria, April 16, 1789, National Archives, Founders Online.
181. George Washington to the Mayor, Corporation, and Citizens of Alexandria, April 16, 1789, National Archives, Founders Online.
182. George Washington to Richard Conway, March 4, 1789, National Archives, Founders Online.
183. George Washington to Richard Conway, March 4, 1789, National Archives, Founders Online.
184. George Washington to Richard Conway, March 4, 1789, National Archives, Founders Online.
185. George Washington to Richard Conway, March 6, 1789, National Archives, Founders Online.
186. George Washington to Richard Conway, March 6, 1789, National Archives, Founders Online.
187. George Washington to Richard Conway, March 6, 1789, National Archives, Founders Online.

## *Chapter 31*

188. "Proclamation, 24 January 1791," National Archives, Founders Online.
189. To George Washington from George Gilpin, January 28, 1791, National Archives, Founders Online; From George Washington to George Gilpin, February 4, 1791, National Archives, Founders Online.
190. Chernow, *Washington*, 704.
191. Chernow, *Washington*, 704.
192. Architect of the Capitol, "First Cornerstone."

193. Chernow, *Washington*, 691.
194. "Neutrality Proclamation, 22 April 1793," National Archives, Founders Online.
195. "Citizens of Alexandria, Virginia, to the President of the United States, The Address of the Inhabitants of Alexandria and its Vicinity, 4 July 1793," National Archives, Founders Online.
196. "Citizens of Alexandria, Virginia, to the President of the United States, The Address of the Inhabitants of Alexandria and its Vicinity, 4 July 1793," National Archives, Founders Online.
197. "Citizens of Alexandria, Virginia, to the President of the United States, The Address of the Inhabitants of Alexandria and its Vicinity, 4 July 1793," National Archives, Founders Online.
198. City of Alexandria, Virginia, "History of Alexandria."
199. Mount Vernon Ladies' Association, George Washington's Mount Vernon Digital Encyclopedia, "Whiskey Rebellion."
200. George Washington to Henry Lee, August 26, 1794, National Archives, Founders Online.
201. George Washington to Henry Lee, August 26, 1794, National Archives, Founders Online.
202. George Washington to Henry Lee, August 26, 1794, National Archives, Founders Online.
203. Mount Vernon Ladies' Association, George Washington's Mount Vernon Digital Encyclopedia, "Whiskey Rebellion."
204. Freeman, *George Washington*, 6:235.
205. Riker, *Fitzgerald's Warehouse, King and Union Streets*.
206. Riker, *Fitzgerald's Warehouse, King and Union Streets*.

## *Chapter 32*

207. Lefkowitz, *George Washington's Indispensable Men*, 195 (Kindle ed.).
208. "September [1795]," National Archives, Founders Online.
209. George Washington to Tobias Lear, November 30, 1795, National Archives, Founders Online.
210. George Washington to Tobias Lear, November 30, 1795, National Archives, Founders Online.
211. Tobias Lear to George Washington, December 14, 1795, National Archives, Founders Online.
212. George Washington to Tobias Lear, March 21, 1796, National Archives, Founders Online.

213. George Washington to Tobias Lear, March 21, 1796, National Archives, Founders Online.
214. George Washington to Tobias Lear, March 21, 1796, National Archives, Founders Online.
215. Tobias Lear to George Washington, March 25, 1796, National Archives, Founders Online.
216. George Washington to Tobias Lear, March 30, 1796, National Archives, Founders Online.
217. George Washington to Tobias Lear, March 30, 1796, National Archives, Founders Online.

## *Chapter 33*

218. Francis Peyton Jr. to George Washington, March 20, 1797, National Archives, Founders Online.
219. Francis Peyton Jr. to George Washington, March 20, 1797, National Archives, Founders Online.
220. Mount Vernon Ladies' Association, George Washington's Mount Vernon Digital Encyclopedia, "William Pearce."
221. George Washington to James Anderson, August 18, 1796, National Archives, Founders Online.
222. John Fitzgerald to George Washington, April 5, 1793, National Archives, Founders Online.
223. George Washington to John Fitzgerald, June 12, 1797, National Archives, Founders Online.
224. George Washington to John Fitzgerald, June 12, 1797, National Archives, Founders Online.
225. John Fitzgerald to George Washington, June 12, 1797, National Archives, Founders Online.
226. John Fitzgerald to George Washington, June 12, 1797, National Archives, Founders Online.
227. Mount Vernon Ladies' Association, George Washington's Mount Vernon Digital Encyclopedia, "Washington's Distillery."
228. Mount Vernon Ladies' Association, George Washington's Mount Vernon Digital Encyclopedia, "Ten Facts About the Distillery."
229. Mount Vernon Ladies' Association, George Washington's Mount Vernon Digital Encyclopedia, "Ten Facts About the Distillery."
230. "Diary entry: 12 February 1798," National Archives, Founders Online.

231. "Diary entry: 12 February 1798," National Archives, Founders Online.
232. George Washington to Sarah Cary Fairfax, May 16, 1798, National Archives, Founders Online.
233. George Washington to Sarah Cary Fairfax, May 16, 1798, National Archives, Founders Online.
234. George Washington to Sarah Cary Fairfax, May 16, 1798, National Archives, Founders Online.
235. USS Constitution Museum, "Quasi-War with France."
236. Old Presbyterian Meeting House Historian provided notes.
237. Old Presbyterian Meeting House Historian provided notes.
238. George Washington to John Adams, July 13, 1798, National Archives, Founders Online.
239. "General Records of the Department of the Navy, 1947–," Guide to Federal Records—Record Group 428, National Archives.
240. "April—1798," National Archives, Founders Online.
241. Washington, *Diaries*, July 4, 1798, National Archives, Founders Online.
242. Washington, *Diaries*, July 4, 1798, National Archives, Founders Online.
243. Washington, *Diaries*, July 4, 1798, National Archives, Founders Online.
244. George Washington to James McHenry, July 27, 1798, National Archives, Founders Online.
245. James McHenry to George Washington, August 13, 1798, National Archives, Founders Online.
246. James McHenry to George Washington, August 13, 1798, National Archives, Founders Online.
247. Washington, *Diaries*, November 5, 1798, National Archives, Founders Online.
248. Washington, *Diaries*, November 5, 1798, National Archives, Founders Online.
249. Washington, *Diaries*, November 5, 1798, National Archives, Founders Online.
250. Chernow, *Washington*, 790.
251. "Candidates for Army Appointments from Virginia," November 1798, National Archives, Founders Online.
252. Washington to McHenry, July 22, 1798, National Archives, Founders Online.
253. Washington, *Diaries*, February 1799, National Archives, Founders Online.
254. Washington, *Diaries*, April 1799, National Archives, Founders Online.
255. Washington, *Diaries*, April 1799, National Archives, Founders Online.
256. Washington, *Diaries*, July 1799, National Archives, Founders Online.
257. George Washington to William Herbert, October 4, 1798, National Archives, Founders Online.
258. William Herbert to George Washington, October 5, 1798, National Archives, Founders Online.

259. George Washington to William Thornton, December 20, 1798, National Archives, Founders Online.
260. Washington, *Diaries*, November 9, 1799, National Archives, Founders Online.
261. George Washington to William Thornton, October 6, 1799, National Archives, Founders Online.
262. George Washington to William Thornton, November 26, 1799, National Archives, Founders Online.
263. Mount Vernon Ladies' Association, George Washington's Mount Vernon Digital Encyclopedia, "Capitol Hill Townhomes."
264. Mount Vernon Ladies' Association, George Washington's Mount Vernon Digital Encyclopedia, "Capitol Hill Townhomes."
265. Washington, *Diaries*, November 1799, National Archives, Founders Online.

## *Chapter 34*

266. Chernow, *Washington*, 807.
267. "I," December 15, 1799, National Archives, Founders Online.

## *Chapter 35*

268. "II," December 14, 1799, National Archives, Founders Online.
269. "George Coryell," memorial no. 19715538, First Presbyterian Church Cemetery, Lambertville, New Jersey, via Find A Grave.
270. "George Washington's Last Will and Testament, 9 July 1799," National Archives, Founders Online.
271. "George Washington's Last Will and Testament, 9 July 1799," National Archives, Founders Online.

## *Epilogue*

272. Virginia Humanities, "Ann Pamela Cunningham."
273. Mount Vernon Ladies' Association, George Washington's Mount Vernon Digital Encyclopedia, "Ann Pamela Cunningham."

# SOURCES

American Battlefield Trust. "Boston Battle Facts and Summary." Revolutionary War Battles, Massachusetts, April 19, 1775–March 17, 1776.

Anderson, Fred. *Crucible of War: The Seven Years' War and the Fate of Empire in British North America, 1754–1766*. Alfred A. Knopf, 2000.

Architect of the Capitol. "First Cornerstone." Explore the Capitol Campus. https://www.aoc.gov/explore-capitol-campus/art/first-cornerstone.

Berlau, John. *George Washington, Entrepreneur: How Our Founding Father's Private Business Pursuits Changed America and the World*. Narrated by Chris Gagne. Macmillan Audio, 2020.

Boyd, Julian P., ed. *The Papers of Thomas Jefferson*. Vol. 5, February 25, 1781–May 20, 1781. Princeton University Press, 1952.

*Brick Chapel to Basilica: A History of Virginia's Oldest Catholic Parish*. Basilica of Saint Mary, Diocese of Arlington, 2024. Printed by AlphaGraphics Old Town Alexandria.

Carlyle House Historic Park, Alexandria, Virginia. John Carlyle image.

Carlyle, J.F., annot. *The Personal and Family Correspondence of Col. John Carlyle of Alexandria, Virginia, 1720–1780*. Northern Virginia Regional Park Authority. https://www.novaparks.com/sites/default/files/John%20Carlyle%201720-1780%20Annotated%20Correspondence_0.pdf.

Chernow, Ron. *Washington: A Life*. Penguin Press, 2010.

City of Alexandria, Virginia. "Alexandria History Museum: George Washington Collection." https://www.alexandriava.gov/museums/alexandria-history-museum-george-washington-collection.

———. "Historic Waterfront, Chapter 1: Founders Park." Alexandria Archaeology Publication (OHA), n.d. https://media.alexandriava.gov/content/oha/reports/HistoricWaterfrontCh1FoundersPark.pdf.

———. "The History of Alexandria: Discovering the Decades." Last modified July 15, 2025. https://www.alexandriava.gov/historic-alexandria/the-history-of-alexandria-discovering-the-decades.

———. "Waterfront History: Princess Street to Queen Street." https://media.alexandriava.gov/docs-archives/historic/info/history/waterfronthistory princesstoqueen.pdf.

Clan Henderson Society of the United States. "History's Hendersons—American Edition." Archived June 10, 2004. https://web.archive.org/web/20040610000512/http://www.clanhendersonusa.org/historyshendersons_us.htm.

Ecelbarger, Gary. "Permanent Losses and New Gains During the 1778 Valley Forge Encampment." *Journal of the American Revolution* (February 15, 2024).

Ellis, Joseph J. *His Excellency: George Washington*. Alfred A. Knopf, 2004.

Fairfax County, Virginia. Deed Book D:693. Fairfax County Courthouse, Fairfax, Virginia.

Freeman, Douglas Southall. *George Washington*. 6 vols. Charles Scribner's Sons, 1948–57.

*George Washington as Colonel in the Virginia Regiment*, by Charles Willson Peale, 1772. Washington-Custis-Lee Collection, Washington and Lee University, Lexington, Virginia. U1897.1.1.

George Washington Masonic National Memorial Association. "A Brief History."

Hand, Tom. "The British Capture Philadelphia." *Americana Corner* blog, January 24, 2023.

*Historic Christ Church*. 3rd ed. Christ Church Gift Shop, printed by Bob's Printing, 2014.

History Committee of the Alexandria Bicentennial. *Notes Prepared by the History Committee of the Alexandria Bicentennial*. Alexandria Library, Local History/Special Collections, vertical file.

Lefkowitz, Arthur S. *George Washington's Indispensable Men: Alexander Hamilton, Tench Tilghman, and the Aides-de-Camp Who Helped Win American Independence*. Stackpole Books, 2020.

Marquis de Lafayette, portrait, by Charles Willson Peale, 1779. Washington-Custis-Lee Collection, Washington and Lee University, Lexington, Virginia.

Martha Dandridge Custis, portrait, by John Wollaston, oil on canvas, 1757. Washington-Custis-Lee Collection, Washington and Lee University, Lexington, Virginia. U1918.1.1.

McCullough, David. *1776*. Simon & Schuster, 2005.

Mount Vernon Ladies' Association. Ann Pamela Cunningham, image. George Washington's Mount Vernon Digital Encyclopedia. https://www.mountvernon.org/library/digitalhistory/digital-encyclopedia/article/ann-pamela-cunningham.

———. Fort Necessity, image. George Washington's Mount Vernon Digital Encyclopedia. https://www.mountvernon.org/library/digitalhistory/digital-encyclopedia/article/fort-necessity.

———. George Mason, image. George Washington's Mount Vernon Digital Encyclopedia. https://www.mountvernon.org/library/digitalhistory/digital-encyclopedia/article/george-mason.

———. George Washington's Mount Vernon Digital Encyclopedia. https://www.mountvernon.org/library/digitalhistory/digital-encyclopedia.

———. Lawrence Washington, image. George Washington's Mount Vernon Digital Encyclopedia. https://www.mountvernon.org/library/digitalhistory/digital-encyclopedia/article/lawrence-washington.

National Archives. "General Records of the Department of the Navy, 1947–." Guide to Federal Records—Record Group 428.

National Constitution Center. "Newburgh Address (1783)." Historic Document Library.

National Park Service. "The George Washington Inaugural Bible." Federal Hall National Memorial.

———. "Health and Medicine." Valley Forge National Historical Park Virtual Museum Exhibit.

———. "Lt Col John Fitzgerald." Valley Forge National Historical Park.

Northern Virginia Regional Parks Authority. "The First Nine Months of 1780: John Carlyle's Last Days." Newsletter, May 2004.

———. John Carlyle (1720–1780), Annotated Correspondence, n.d. https://www.novaparks.com/sites/default/files/John%20Carlyle%201720-1780%20Annotated%20Correspondence_0.pdf.

———. "The Ties That Bind: How Influential Family Connections and Initiative Gave Rise to William Fairfax's Prominence in Virginia." Extra Edition, May 2009.

O'Keefe, Kieran J. "The American Revolution in Alexandria, Virginia: Upheaval in George Washington's Hometown." *Journal of the American Revolution* (October 13, 2020). https://allthingsliberty.com/2020/10/the-american-revolution-in-alexandria-virginia-upheaval-in-george-washingtons-hometown.

Pennsylvania Historical & Museum Commission and WITF Inc. "Excerpts from the Diary of Colonel John Fitzgerald on Washington's Crossing of the Delaware, December 25–26, 1776." Explore PA History.

Preisser, Thomas M. "Eighteenth-Century Alexandria, Virginia, before the Revolution, 1749–1776." Master's thesis, College of William & Mary, 1977. Paper 1539623705. https://dx.doi.org/10.21220/s2-9jf6-s176.

Riker, Diane. *Fitzgerald's Warehouse, King and Union Streets*. Alexandria Archaeology Studies of the Old Waterfront. Office of Historic Alexandria, City of Alexandria, 2008.

Rowland, Kate Mason. *The Life of George Mason, 1725–1792: Including His Speeches, Public Papers, and Correspondence*. 2 vols. G.P. Putnam's Sons, 1892.

Sinks, John D. "The Life and Times of Physician-General William Brown." Fairfax Resolves Chapter, Sons of the American Revolution, December 17, 1999.

Terrell, Timothy G. "The Fairfax Militia During the Revolutionary War Period." Arlington Historical Society, February 2020.

Virginia Humanities. "Ann Pamela Cunningham (August 15, 1816–May 1, 1875)." *Encyclopedia Virginia*.

Washington, George. *A Plan of Alexandria, Now Belhaven* (1749). Map. https://www.loc.gov/item/98687108.

———. *Plat of the Land Where on Stands the Town of Alexandria* (1748). Map. https://www.loc.gov/item/99466767.

White, William E. "The Independent Companies of Virginia, 1774–1775." *Virginia Magazine of History and Biography* 86, no. 2 (1978): 149–62. http://www.jstor.org/stable/4248201.

Woodward, Colin. "Henry Lee (1756–1818)." *Encyclopedia Virginia*, December 7, 2020.

USS Constitution Museum. "The Quasi-War with France (1798–1801)." https://ussconstitutionmuseum.org/major-events/the-quasi-war-with-france.

# INDEX

## D



## E



## F



## G

## N



## O



## P



## Q



## R



## S

## T



## V



## W



## Y

# ABOUT THE AUTHOR

Tim Rose is the founder of Alexansdria History Tours, a veteran- and locally owned tour company in Old Town Alexandria, Virginia. Tim served as an infantry officer in the U.S. Marine Corps from 2011 to 2021. He is passionate about Alexandria's ties to George Washington and the city's role in the French and Indian War, Revolutionary War, and Civil War. He lives in Alexandria with his family, and together they enjoy spending time in Old Town and at Mount Vernon.